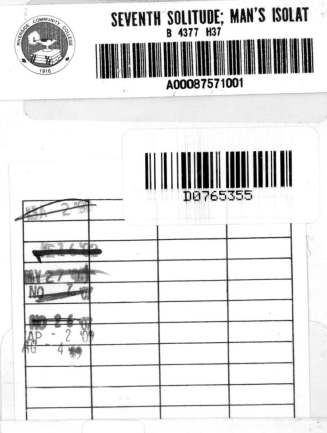

THE SEVENTH SOLITUDE

THE SEVENTH SOLITUDE

Man's Isolation in
Kierkegaard, Dostoevsky,
and Nietzsche

by

RALPH HARPER

THE JOHNS HOPKINS PRESS
Baltimore, Maryland

This book has been brought to publication with
the assistance of a grant from The Ford Foundation.

Preface

THIS IS A BOOK about some of the features of spiritual homelessness, a book about ideas of solitude even more than about solitary men. Mankind has not always had to breathe in the thin air of Nietzschean solitude. The man from whom Nietzsche himself said he had learned, Stendhal, would feel rather out of place in the twentieth century, his ambience being geographical and artistic rather than metaphysical. But Stendhal's contemporary, Kierkegaard, was the first to see clearly the two radical alternatives confronting man: eternity or despair. Nietzsche and Dostoevsky are in truth his inheritors, each adding his own weighted understanding of these two options.

Although Dostoevsky held within his own personality as well as in his fiction all of Nietzsche's nihilism, Dostoevsky himself remained partly safe, spiritually safe on the threshold between the Christian world and the world of self-destruction. And so it is not Dostoevsky who says the last word—it is Nietzsche, as does anyone who shuts the door tight against all other alternatives. For this reason Dostoevsky can be more helpful to us who would seek a way out of the world of Nietzsche in which we have been placed. And if, after careful consideration, we conclude that Dostoevsky was too close to Nietzsche in spirit to draw us high and dry out of the Nietzschean vortex, we may at length take heart from the nostalgia as much as from the honesty of Dostoevsky, who, knowing the implications of a world in which God is silent, kept on hammering against the iron gates. We may still be able to do something he had no time for: return to the dead ends of nihilism and search its chambers for unnoticed exits.

RALPH HARPER

Monkton, Md.
Summer 1964

Acknowledgments

I WISH TO ACKNOWLEDGE the translations I have used in quoting from the works of Dostoevsky, Kafka, Kierkegaard, Nietzsche, Pascal, Proust, St. Augustine, and Stendhal.

For the writings of Dostoevsky, except for *The Possessed*, I have quoted from the Constance Garnett translations, published by Macmillan, Random House (Modern Library), and Dell. I have used the Andrew MacAndrew translation of *The Possessed*, published in 1962 by the New American Library of World Literature, Inc. (Signet).

The quotations from Kafka's *The Castle* are taken from the Knopf edition of 1954, translated by Willa and Edwin Muir.

I have used the Princeton University Press editions of Kierkegaard, translated by Walter Lowrie, David F. and Lillian M. Swenson, and edited by Alexander Dru.

The quotations from Nietzsche's *Twilight of the Idols* and *Anti-Christ* are from Walter Kaufmann's translations in the *Viking Portable Nietzsche*, published in 1954. Other quotations are from the Modern Library Giant edition and a 1909 edition edited by Oscar Levy.

I have used J. M. Cohen's translations of Pascal's *Pensées*, in the Penguin edition of 1961.

For Proust, I have quoted from the C. K. Scott-Moncrieff translation of *Remembrance of Things Past*, published by Random House in 1934. I have also used Frederick A. Blossom's translation of the final novel, *The Past Remembered*.

The quotations of St. Augustine's *Confessions* are from the F. J. Sheed translation, published in 1943 by Sheed & Ward, New York, N.Y.

And for Stendhal, I have quoted from the C. K. Scott-Moncrieff translations of *The Charterhouse of Parma* (published by Liveright) and *The Red and the Black* (published by Random House, Modern Library) and from H. L. R. Edwards' translation of Lucien Leuwen (published by John Lehmann, London, 1951).

Contents

CHAPTER 1

The Night of Absolutes

*"He who cannot endure the sentence, 'There is
no redemption' ought to die out."*—Nietzsche

NIETZSCHE WOULD NOT HAVE appreciated Kafka's *The Castle,* story of
a man in whom God is not completely dead. He would have said, why
should one try to get permission to live? Resign yourself to being "a
stranger, a man who isn't wanted and is in everybody's way" (Kafka).
But either God really has receded (Heidegger), or is malevolent
(Epicurus), or is a practical joker who hides himself and contrives to
frustrate the very people who want to obey him. Kafka's tormented
task, to which he dedicated his life, was to contemplate this evasive
possibility. It was not Nietzsche's task. Nor could he feel as guilt
the spiritual solitude that overwhelmed Kafka. They were both "homeless ones" living in a "frail, broken-down, transition period," but one
had an uneasy conscience, and the other claimed to be cheerful.

> The background of our cheerfulness . . . . The greatest recent
> event—that God is dead that the belief in the Christian God has
> ceased to be believable . . . . The consequences for us—not at all
> sad and dark, but rather like a new, scarcely describable kind of
> light, happiness, relief, exhilaration, encouragement, dawn—our
> heart overflows with gratitude, amazement, anticipation, expecta-
> tion (because the old God is dead)—the horizon appears free
> again to us, even granted that it is not bright.

Perhaps Nietzsche was not so cheerful in actuality, but he thought he
should be.

There are two sources of solitude and its agony: being cut off from
other men and being cut off from God. Kafka and Nietzsche knew

both. And yet they knew them in different ways. Kafka did not want to be cut off from other people—he yearned to belong. There were dark, discouraging moments in Nietzsche's life when he too wished for friends who could understand him; but he never wanted to belong. Kafka, like Kirillov, feared that God might not exist, and that at best God would notice man if only by crushing him. Nietzsche, so far as we know, at no time considered that God was anything but an out-worn and debilitating idea; and while he could feel the solitude of a man who must think everything out from scratch, he scrupulously avoided praying for comfort or release. One of the most impressive things about him is his integrity. "No pain has been and shall be able to tempt me into giving false testimony about life as I recognize it."

Nietzsche dissolved nothing that his few readers did not already recognize was dissolving. And if he convinces now, it is not because his arguments are watertight—how can anyone prove non-existence?—but because he set side by side three components of man's despair: first, a series of suggestions as to the reasons why men have wanted to believe in God; second, a list of absolutes that the word God has come to stand for; and third, the psychological consequences of unbelief, consequences already felt. What he liked to call his "natural history of morals" might better be called "natural history of absolutes." He knew them all, and was unwilling to uphold the unyoked humor of their idleness. Once delivered from their miasma, he asked himself and others to look at reality with new eyes, and, if possible, cheerfully.

Nietzsche thought that God had been needed for three reasons. Men fear to suffer, and would like to think that death will be not only the end of earthly suffering but the beginning of heavenly joy. God and heaven would guarantee this. Some men resent the natural and acquired superiority of others; it would be consoling to think that by being passive they could earn the acclaim that birth or activity had not earned for them. God is needed to recognize such an inverted rating. And finally, born into a world which all too often defies explanation, mankind has concluded that "any explanation is better than none," and that God is needed as ultimate although invisible explainer.

Is it not likely then that man, having such good reasons to invent God, should have done so? The results seem to confirm the suspicion.

Whatever the theological system, the shape is the same: there is a world behind or above the world experienced, and it has purpose and unity. Man, therefore, cannot be utterly lonely; his task will be, like Kafka's, to make the right contacts with the unseen world, and, if necessary, propitiate it. At this point Nietzsche does not argue; he states, in effect, "but that is not the way it is at all." Man invents, not discovers, truth; there is nothing to discover but what one already sees. There are no absolutes, no antitheses of seen and unseen, appearance and reality, being and becoming. The very idea of antitheses testifies to man's fear of solitude, and man's inventive power. The plausibility of Nietzsche's attitude rests ultimately on the very fears that he said brought the opposite idea, God, into history.

Another world, "a true world," with its transcendental objects (Platonic ideas), is "indemonstrable and unattainable." What began in desperation has become a fable. Since there is no creator, there can be no separate creation: "the universe exists; it is nothing that grows in existence and that passes out of existence." Facts and phenomena are only facts and phenomena. There are, therefore, no moral phenomena, only moral interpretations of phenomena. The idea of truth as independent of the mind is itself a fiction: logic is fiction, truth a lie. The idea of purpose as independent of resolution and planning is likewise a fiction. Nothing is intrinsically desirable or worthwhile; we are what we make ourselves to be. Life and events do not have meaning; they are to be given meaning. This is, admittedly, nihilism, and "thorough nihilism is the conviction that life is absurd." He sums up his "doctrine" as follows: "No one is responsible for man's being here at all . . . for his being such and such, or for his being in these circumstances or in this environment . . . . Man is not the effect of some special purpose, of a will and end . . . . We have invented the concept of 'end': in reality there is no end." And there is no resurrection either. "When one places life's center of gravity not in life but in the beyond—in nothingness—one deprives life of its center of gravity altogether." There was "only one Christian and he died on the cross." (Kirillov had said the same.)

The consequences are upon us, Nietzsche said. "When we have sought in all that has happened a purpose that is not there, the seeker will lose courage." And when we lose a sense of unity behind the diversity of experience, we lose confidence in our own importance. Indeed, if "the reality of becoming is the only reality that is admitted," the world itself appears worthless. What is left? For what can man live? How can he justify reality? How can man endure? At no time did Nietzsche doubt that these are real questions. He accepted the apparent need for self-justification. But his answer was unambiguously clear and hard. "What justifies man is his reality—it will eternally justify him." "Existence itself is sufficiently holy to justify an enormous amount of suffering." Therefore, a man should "say *yes* to the whole cosmic economy which justifies the terrible, the evil, and the questionable." The more terrifying the circumstances of life, the better for man, so that his freedom, power, and imagination can be tested to the breaking point, to find out "whether he is in any need of a faith at the end." "If he required a God in the past, he now delights in cosmic disorder without a God, a world of accident."

From here on Nietzsche's manner sounds a little forced. "Excelsior! . . . You will never pray again, never adore again, never again rest in endless trust . . . no stopping before ultimate wisdom, ultimate goodness, ultimate power . . . you have no perpetual guardian and friend for your seven solitudes . . . . Do you want to renounce all this? Who will give you the necessary strength? Nobody yet has had this strength." Nor had Nietzsche. If he was right, then there ought to have been a new dawn, new horizons, an open sea. Man ought to feel cheerful; his logic ought to be gay. But Nietzsche did not have the strength or the imagination to invent anything new, and had to fall back on what had already been—he clothed its drabness by calling it eternal recurrence. And for the last eleven years of his life, with body paralyzed and mind benumbed, he stared and stared at what had been. The life which he dreamed of as "the Great Noon: a moment of supreme self-consciousness," turned out for him to be a dead end. He sat in "uncanny silence . . . solitude has seven skins; nothing can penetrate it." He had become his own best symbol.

CHAPTER 2

Self-Isolation

"To transform the world, to recreate it afresh, man must turn into another path psychologically . . . but first we have to go through a period of isolation."—Dostoevsky

SOLITUDE IS NOT NEW. There have always been men and women born to be lonely. Others have even chosen loneliness. Heroes and saints, for example, have taken loneliness for granted as part of the price to be paid for the honor or the holiness they sought. The sick and the talented could console themselves by saying that it is not their fault. The clowns and the criminals also chose to be different and expected laughter or indignation. Only one kind of man has so deliberately transformed himself so as to stand apart from normal expectation. Stendhal called him *"étranger,"* which we translate inadequately as stranger, foreigner, outsider. To Kierkegaard the outsider was "the individual" or "the wild goose"; to Dostoevsky he was a "double" or "Titan"; to Nietzsche a "free spirit" or "superman."

Whatever the beginning of his solitude, an outsider knows he is not like most men; and the knowledge of his difference hurts. The nineteenth and twentieth centuries in art and real life have left a frieze of outsiders of all kinds, ranging from epic and tragic heroes to orphans and refugees. They are all brothers in a communion of displacement and loneliness with the departed and unseen solitaries of the past. There is one exception, the new self-conscious solitude of those who record the absence or silence of God. To be homeless and in exile is as old and sad as the hills; to be metaphysically homeless and to care is new.

5

Kierkegaard would have preferred, romantically considered, to have been a police spy rather than a martyr, and Nietzsche said he would rather be a clown (he was) than a saint (he was not). Dostoevsky, less hopefully, would rather have been a holy elder than a buffoon. All three feared and respected their kinship with Don Quixote, "ever threatened by ignominious denial of oneself at the end of one's striving" (Dostoevsky). They shared an inability—or unwillingness—to run with the pack. They had not been rejected, and they did not want to belong. They did the rejecting themselves, scorning "the crowd" (Kierkegaard), "the idea of God" (Dostoevsky), "European morality" (Nietzsche). It is unimaginable that Kierkegaard, Dostoevsky, or Nietzsche would have anything but scorn for Thomas Mann's "artist with a bad conscience" who with Tonio Kröger could whine: "I stand between two worlds. I am at home in neither, and I suffer in consequence. . . . My deepest and secretest love belongs to the blond and blue-eyed, the fair and living, the happy, lovely, and commonplace." With all their strength and with all their contempt they rejected the commonplace (and would have rejected James Joyce along with it). Born different, they accepted the challenge of those who caution, "Be like us, and you will be safe." They preferred to be unsafe and unhappy for the sake of passion and honesty.

Each in his own way was a critic of modernity, owing no allegiance to anyone or anything. Each presents himself to a would-be biographer as an enigma preoccupied with man the enigma. There are many and subtle differences between them and the characters they created; in a biography or work of literary criticism it is important to distinguish and dissect. But for the purpose of examining and relating their ideas, it is convenient and, I think, not unjust to identify the author with some of his characters, leaving aside the masks and ironies that, indeed, not even a biographer can finally be sure of. Ivan Karamazov was to his brother Dmitri "a tomb." But so was man to St. Augustine "an abyss." Dostoevsky and Nietzsche likewise were tombs, and we must think of them as Kierkegaard's secretary said of his employer: "Anyone who wishes to deal with S.K.'s life must take care not to burn his fingers—it is so full of contradictions—so difficult to get to the bottom of that man of moods." It is safer to stick to their ideas, and to confess openly that when I say "Dostoevsky says," or "Kierkegaard thought," I am using a convention that gives the ideas some sanction but does not resolve the degree of commitment of their spokesman to them. After all, which of our ideas can be completely identified with any of us?

These authors make uneasy reading. Sometimes they exasperate us, at other times we laugh at them. Sometimes they make us feel judged; at other times they force us to reconsider our fondest preconceptions. They are intensely self-conscious and value-conscious; to read them is to be encouraged by example to be like them. When Dostoevsky describes (in *Nyetochka Nyesvanovna*) the appearance of someone as "a desperate, feverish contest between violently over-strained will and inner impotence—always rapid in his transitions," we recognize the manner of the author himself. This manner leads to humiliations for Dostoevsky (insult and injury), to abysmal melancholy for Kierkegaard, to iron-bound depression for Nietzsche. They are always on the edge of nervous collapse; their style and example are catching. They blow both hot and cold (no Laodiceans they), are intemperate and rigorous, humorous and sober, dogmatic and yet observant. They are philosopher-artists, living out a Pascalian wager, gambling all or nothing.

Take Nietzsche, the would-be sage, perpetually in motion, walking in the hills, singing as he walked, talking aloud to himself, washing and re-washing his hands, following the sun from resort to resort, drinking water and medicines for indigestion, headaches, and blindness—yet gentle, courteous, painfully shy. Dostoevsky, epileptic; Kierkegaard, hunchback, inhibited by nature, exhibitionist by intent. Raskolnikov might have been speaking for them all when he said, "I want to become a Napoleon, to overstep boundaries." Kierkegaard had already written:

> The fact that Napoleon always carried poison about with him is really an expression of the desperate energy with which he lived. In the meanwhile that is something by comparison with the bestial dullness and habitual security in which most men

doze—until they die. It is really not worth bothering oneself with men except with those who have given their life for something or at least have religious or desperate energy enough to think of death everyday.

Stendhal had said that only a sentence of death distinguishes a man. Of course, he was mistaken; it is the one thing all have in common. But Kierkegaard, too, writing in a time when men had forgotten what it is to die, along with forgetting what it means to exist, said that he preferred to read books only by those condemned to death.

The thriller as we know it today had scarcely begun in the middle of the nineteenth century, but we can see the beginning of a need for it in Stendhal's passion for pseudonyms and conspiracy, his pretense that he was wanted by the Austrian police, in Kierkegaard's equally romantic "desire to be in the police. It seemed to me a fitting occupation for my sleepless, intriguing mind [we might insert "pseudonymous mind"]. I imagined that among criminals there were people worth fighting with, clever, crafty, desperate men. Later on I recognized that it was a good thing that I gave up the idea; for almost everything the police have to deal with, is concerned with poverty and misery—not criminals or gangsters." Nietzsche too affected to admire "the criminal type—the type of the strong man who has been made sick . . . whose virtues are put in ban by society, our domesticated, mediocre, emasculated society in which a man with his natural forces unimpaired, coming from the mountains or from sea-faring adventures necessarily degenerates into a criminal . . . . The Corsican Napoleon is the most celebrated case." And then he goes on to say that "the testimony of Dostoevsky is of importance," because he had lived with "capital criminals . . . persons carved almost out of the best, the hardest, and the most valuable material to be found in the Russian dominions." Dostoevsky had no such illusions about criminals or about criminal ideas. Unlike Nietzsche, however, he could feel the twisted motives of the criminal inside himself.

Gamblers, artists in conspiracy, improvisers, they could see their destiny in the nineteenth century as hemmed in by two moats, with mediocrity on one side and God on the other. On the narrow plain between the moats gambling tables have been set up, lovely ladies look on, and in a moment everything is to be decided forever. They are theatrical one moment, deacon-sober the next. "Have your masks and your ruses, that ye may be mistaken for what you are, or somewhat feared," says Nietzsche. "Everything that is profound loves the mask." If they did not fool themselves into thinking they had undisclosed names and depths, they have fooled almost all their readers. Perhaps they were just what they showed, perhaps, to use Nietzsche's manner of speaking, there was no Being behind the Becoming; their masks were their faces. Dostoevsky uses no pseudonyms, unless Svidrigailov, Versilov, Stavroguin, Alyosha, and all the others are his pseudonyms. They represent his secret quests and dilemmas. But sooner or later we find that at bottom they are as clear and simple as the trout on the floor of the pool after the swirl and mud have settled. They are the author's way of holding his reader's attention; something terrible is going to happen—it does not always—or we shall at last find out what Stavroguin or Versilov is. But when we do, it does not matter, as it does not matter when Kierkegaard tells us what we have known all along, that he wrote his own books. "Not one word of the pseudonymous works is mine . . . I have no opinion about them except as a third person." Only the most slavish Kierkegaardian would not admit that his master unconscionably wasted time pretending (not trying) to woo his obtuse reading public. A man who insists too often, "I am only a poet," "I am not a Christian, but I know what Christianity is," may end by being believed.

The case of Kierkegaard—he forces the clinical term upon us—is instructive. He asked to be judged as a wild goose, by his indifference to the world. But he was one of the most thin-skinned men ever to have lived, and was abnormally *not* "indifferent" to the world. He held that his suffering constituted his superiority, and that he, like the martyrs of old, was suffering for the doctrine. The question is, what doctrine? Although he wrote movingly of the Incarnation and of God's love for man and man's double love for God and man in turn, the doctrine he always had in mind when he talked of suffering was simply the doctrine of a martyr's suffering. It is hard to escape the suspicion that he sought extraordinary suffering for its own sake and held it close in spite of every opportunity— marriage and career—to avoid it. "If I had had faith," he said, "I would have married her." Faith in what? Perhaps he loved Regine Olson: but he loved his melancholy more. Asthete, man-about-town, he talked romantically about becoming a country parson. A vocation isolated enough no doubt, but Kierkegaard wanted his self-isolation even more.

The lines of his "case" can be found in *Sickness unto Death*, and this book more than all the others rings with sobriety and contemporaneity today. Kierkegaard was never more eloquent or more exact than when he wrote of despair; he knew this from the heart. He may have been "a knight of hidden inwardness," with a faith that could move mountains. But he moved no mountains, and this is the only evidence we know to look for. He wrote of his own self-isolation as a form of the demoniacal, and admitted that salvation depended on his breaking out. In 1848, one year after he had written the meditation, *Works of Love,* he experienced a religious crisis which prompted him to say in his journal on the Wednesday before Easter, "My whole being is changed. My reserve and self-isolation is broken—I must speak. Lord, give thy grace. . . . Alas, she could not break the silence of my melancholy . . . Now with God's help I shall be myself, I believe that Christ will help me to be victorious over my melancholy, and so I shall become a priest." Five days later he had to take it all back. "No, no, my self-isolation cannot be broken, at least not now. The thought of breaking it occupies me so much, and at all times, that it only becomes more and more firmly embedded."

Nothing he subsequently offered as an explanation makes much sense of this about-face. He tried to say that his self-isolation was a punishment for his father's sin when, as a child, he cursed God on a Jutland heath. This in itself is far-fetched; his father had already asked for forgiveness. What did he want to be eternally punished for—so that he could justify rejecting the forgiveness he insisted he believed in? "To be sure, I believe in the forgiveness of sins, but I understand it as hitherto, that I must bear my punishment all my life, of remaining in the painful prison of my isolation, in a profound sense cut off from communication with other men." No youthful moral lapse, not even his cruelly selfish rejection of Regine Olson could justify shutting himself outside forgiveness. He would have said that he believed in forgiveness, but not enough to believe that he could be forgiven. More likely he knew that he did not want to be forgiven at all, for then, like the man "in despair at willing to be himself," he might have to find another self to be.

WHO AM I?

How much does the isolated man know about himself? Stendhal, apostle of self-knowledge, was never quite sure. "Who am I?" asks Lucien Leuwen, "The truth is, I don't know what I am and I'd give a lot if anyone would enlighten me." The young Kierkegaard had also wondered, "What I really lack is to be clear in my mind what I am to do, not what I am to know. The thing is to understand myself, to see what God really wishes me to do, the thing is to find a truth which is true for me." The words are full of ethical purpose, but the concern behind them is self-regarding. Kierkegaard journeyed to the interior and never came back. "What is the truth for me?" And he goes on to assume that when he discovers that truth, it will be so private that it will be incommunicable. No wonder that the equally self-enclosed Nietzsche could say, "At the absurdly tender age of seven, I already knew that no human speech would ever reach me;" there was no human speech worth listening to, coming from the herd, the crowd. Kierkegaard admitted that he was "an unhappy individuality which from its earliest years has been nailed fast to some suffering or other bordering on madness." There is much that is interchangeable between these two writers. They were, to paraphrase Stendhal, unhappy men at war with the whole of society, and with themselves. They were "*étranger*" to all accepted attitudes, and accordingly, aliens in their own lands. Born different they were, but they accepted their difference with a challenge. As Kierkegaard put it, "I am by nature so polemically constituted that I only fee. myself really in my element when I am surrounded by human mediocrity and paltriness." Unfortunately the challenge comes out as contempt.

The new category—at least Kierkegaard and Nietzsche claimed it was new—is the individual, "capable of creating new things." And yet creation by rhetoric was all either could look forward to. They knew much about genius which, "like a thunderstorm comes up against the wind" (Kierkegaard), and about great men who are "dangerous, accidents, exceptions, tempests which are strong enough to question things which it has taken time to build and establish." They themselves probably destroyed nothing, but they certainly participated in dissolution and picked up no pieces. In the end Nietzsche's definition of greatness is equally applicable to himself, Kierkegaard, and many of Dostoevsky's heroes: "The man is great who knows how to be most solitary," "the man who is surrounded by loneliness, not because he wishes to be alone, but because he is what he is, and cannot find his equal." But why should solitude make a man great? They do not say. There is no more moving passage in Nietzsche than the following: King Among Insects

> Alone I confront a tremendous problem. It is a forest in which I lose myself, a virgin forest. I need help. I need disciples. I need a master. To obey would be sweet. If I had lost myself on a mountain, I would obey the men who knew that mountain, and if I should meet a man capable of enlightening me on moral ideas, I would listen to him, I would follow him. But I find no one, no disciples and fewer masters . . . I am alone.

Is it any wonder that oppressed by his solitude, forgetting that it was his greatness, he should have pretended that he was really writing for real people, a happy few? "When I found it necessary to, I invented the free spirits. There are no free spirits, nor have there been, but I then required them for company to keep me cheerful in the midst of evils." Poor, honest soul, there were times when he would boast that no human speech had ever reached him, there were times when he would admit that he was lost in the world of men.

"As a stranger, a proscribed man, I wander among them; never a word, never a look now reaches me . . . it is terrible to be condemned to silence when one has so many things to say. Am I created for solitude, never to find anyone with whom I may make myself understood?" Incommunicability is in truth the most awful of solitudes. Take this cup from me. He knew that "a profound man needs friends, unless he has a God. And I have neither God nor friend." Cut off from friends, God, traditional acceptances, he had only his own empty self to fall back on, a self yearning to be great but having nothing but denial to be great about.

REASON AND NATURE

Without home or law the superman has only instinct and reason to depend on. But instinct is treacherous; it leads too often to union with others and the end of isolation. Sensibility and the reasons of the heart break down the consciousness of individuality. Reason, on the other hand, should be servant not master. This was a presupposition of Dostoevsky's heroes as well as of Nietzsche. The former knew that reason had limitations too. "Reason is an excellent thing," says the Underground Man, "but reason is nothing but reason and satisfied by the rational side of man's nature, while will is a manifestation of the whole life . . . including reason and all the impulses."

Reason is not a world, but an instrument to use in the world. The more analytical the rationalist becomes, the less easy it is for him to appreciate the individuality of others. And yet his intellectual exercises convince him of his own distinguished individuality. Just as reason protects self-interest, so sex is the arena where self-interest faces its severest test. Sex is a natural barrier which, added to other differences between men and women, is sometimes too alien to be overcome. A certain type of man—for example, Kierkegaard, Nietzsche, Stavroguin—may want love and yet be unable to give or accept it. What they want is recognition of themselves, and it is little wonder that their flirtations should conclude in estrangement.

Nietzsche's encounter with the brilliant Lou Salome may have convinced him that it was better "not to cleave to any person, be it even the dearest—every person is a prison and also a recess." This reminds us of Simone Weil's pathetic conviction: "I feel that it is necessary and ordained that I should be alone, a stranger and an exile in relation to every human circle without exception." And she too was alone.

Women are mirrors in which some men can see themselves more clearly. Occasionally they find someone innocent or religious enough to be impervious to the disease of isolation that has weakened the men. Stendhal's Julien Sorel, for example, loves two kinds of women, one to satisfy his pride and the other his humility. Dostoevsky's heroines, living in a society in which inertia can be avoided only by a show of aristocratic defiance or by its opposite, meekness, let their lives be woven with the needs men have for them. In this sense they are reflections of men. Only the man who has pity in him, like Raskolnikov, can find a Sonia (Sophia) interesting, and only someone rebellious, like Ivan, can find a Katerina Ivanovna lovable. But however much these men want these women, they find it impossible to be at ease with them.

Kierkegaard, who uttered the outsider's truism, "Community will not save us," could not be saved by love or isolation either. And even when two young people are suited to each other, their relationship may sicken because they cannot be spontaneous; they must play a role. The very people who over-praise spontaneity are the ones who rate recognition more highly still. "Passionate love," says Stendhal, "was far more a model which they were imitating than a reality with them." If they do not actually detest each other before long, they are bound to discover sooner or later what the Underground Man knew so well, that "loving meant tyrannizing and showing my moral superiority." The lover is, to recall Sartre's phrase, "an alien freedom." The young Stendhal, with illusions about politics as well as love, could ask, "While the entire youth of France takes sides in such great causes, am I going to spend my life gazing into a pair of beautiful eyes?" He came to believe that this should be his destiny, and regretted that it was not. The great distance from

Stendhal at the beginning of the century to Nietzsche at the end can be measured by the latter's apparent indifference to "a pair of beautiful eyes." It was what Nietzsche needed, even more than Stendahl.

Where community and sex both fail, a man can often fall back on the natural affection and care of his family. In the end Nietzsche had to do this. Kierkegaard was troubled all his life by memory of a "crazy upbringing" by his father; and Dostoevsky, whose father had been murdered by his serfs, was abnormally preoccupied with the relationships between children and irresponsible parents. Ivan Karamazov, brought up as an orphan by relatives, is the one who says that there is "no natural law to love." Dostoevsky wondered whether reason could then take its place, and he concluded that it could not. In *The Brothers Karamazov*, he imagined three kinds of fatherhood, that of old Karamazov the sensualist, the holy elder Zossima, and the sentimental weakling Snegiryov. Karamazov has never loved his sons and is not loved by them, and is murdered by his "natural" son, with the connivance of Ivan and the open and secret approval of Dmitri and Alyosha. Zossima loves this Alyosha as his father ought to have loved him, and Alyosha loves the boys of the town as he himself is loved, especially Ilusha Snegiryov, whose father has been insulted and humiliated by Dmitri. And the elder Snegiryov loves his Ilusha although he has done nothing to earn his son's respect. It is not true, therefore, as Alyosha thinks, that "everyone hates his father." But when natural love is shattered by a father like Karamazov, the sons can resent his indifference so greatly that they assume that what is true for them is true for all. And so like the defense lawyer at Dmitri's trial, they may ask, "Why am I bound to love him?" And they will not hear the Johannine answer, "Because he first loved us." No, they must ask their fathers,

"Father, tell me, why must I love you? Father, show me that I must love you;" and if that father is able to answer him and show him good reason, we have a real, normal, parental relation, not resting on mystical prejudice, but on a rational, responsible and strictly humanitarian basis. But if he does not, there is an end to the family tie. He is not a father to him, and the son has a right to look upon him as a stranger and even an enemy.

If there is no natural law to love, if a father cannot love his children without reason, naturally, can reason be a substitute? Hardly. Dostoevsky summed this up when he said, "Those accursed families in which there is neither love nor God . . . and where there is no love, there is no sense either." Pathetic though Stavroguin's vague hope for redemption through Liza, it is much less pathetic than Arkady Dolgoruky's (*The Raw Youth*) ingenuous plea to his "natural" father Versilov to recognize his as a son. A natural orphan is not the most solitary of human beings; the metaphysically homeless is more desolate.

TO BE A STRANGER IS MY LOT

Is the *raison d'être étranger* to be "an observer of the human heart" whose greatest satisfaction is, according to Stendhal, in dreaming? Or is it to be a poet, as Kierkegaard suggested, speaking with his own voice and lacking God's authority? Even Kierkegaard was sure that he had given "so exact a description of Christianity and its relation to the world that a young man with enthusiasm and nobility of mind will be able to find it on a map." Whether life is identified with a *récherche du bonheur, chasse au bonheur, promesse de bonheur,* it is an instinct that rejects all obligations to others and postulates a duty to oneself. Is it any surprise that love so seldom succeeds? Julien Sorel's "I owe it to myself to be her lover" is scarcely considerate or persuasive. Whoever is looking for "inner rights," like Raskolnikov, for whom "mere existence is too little," builds all on "the calm and solitary consciousness of strength." The Napoleonic instinct to exert this strength over everyone else is the sort of nobility admired by Nietzsche as well as by Raskolnikov. It is exertion for the sake of exertion, nobility without obligation. When Julien Sorel says, "I owe it to myself to attack this woman," he does not mean merely, "I owe it to myself to be a conqueror among women as Napoleon was among nations." He is looking for an environment where he can flourish. Ostensibly and instinctively as well, he detests the conventional and insensible, and yet underneath he desires spontaneity and association: the natural. The self would like to meet another like itself; spontaneity would like to meet the spontaneous. But in Nietzsche's mind the unexpected is idolized at first for its own sake. His "will to power" is spontaneity minus any arena in which to exercise. And this is why his principle of novelty has finally to be fused with his discovery of sameness, Eternal Recurrence. Nietzsche was made uneasy not only by the commonplace, but by what Stendhal called "the charm of the unexpected." As Henri de Lubac has justly said, Nietzsche felt "an immeasurable lack of satisfaction with every aspect of being." He only touched on life, as he wandered from *pension* to *pension*. And his vaunted admiration for energy was curiously contentless and generalized.

Having scorned gregariousness and sought solitude, traded equality for distinction, hypocrisy for sincerity, the outsider's conscience is quiet until he tries to find new values to replace the old. When he finds he cannot get out of the compulsive whirligig of self-will, his troubles begin. The strain of inspiration is too great, and he even tires of his own sincerity. He who had begun with the exemplar Napoleon may end with a quixotic recantation. But wisdom comes late, after the individual is burned out. Nietzsche was to confide, "I will not conceal it from you; things are going badly with me. Night more and more surrounds me. It is as if there had just been a flash of lightning; now it is over." All his life he had tried to live on an image instead of on the available concreteness of nature. He had pretended that other people have dignity only when they recognized his significance. He could give pronouncements, but not himself. Even his visions were windblown. "I once saw a storm raging over the sea and a clear blue sky above it; it was then that I came to dislike all sunless, cloudy passions which know no light, except the lightning." Light, energy, a solitude flashing before darkness settles —only the unexpected could have saved him. He could not reach out until it was too late: "I love thee, Ariadne."

No one understood the role of dreams and images better than Dostoevsky. His hero Raskolnikov, before putting a crude Nietzscheism into practice, dreamed that he saw a peasant beating a horse and that he had tried to protect the poor beast by embracing its head. He himself, perfectly awake, coolly went out and beat an old woman to death. When Nietzsche collapsed in a Turin street, he was found weeping on the neck of a horse that was being beaten. The human soul is more profound than its pride and consciousness, more powerful even than its most compassionate dreams. But it may at times only be able to assert its recognition of human dignity through madness.

CHAPTER 3

Hidden Inwardness

"There is hardly one man in a generation who is profound enough to have, or unfortunate enough to be obliged to have a hidden inwardness. . . . But stop a moment! It is to a certain extent true of me that I was unfortunate enough to go about and conceal a hidden inwardness."—Kierkegaard

WHEN NIETZSCHE SAYS THAT man must be surpassed, he means man in the nineteenth century. To neither Stendhal at the beginning of the century nor Nietzsche at the end did it ever occur, apparently, that the very nature of man is problematical at all times. This is what makes Kierkegaard's witness fresh. He recalled to his contemporaries the possibility of their having a conscience that most of them had forgotten, and he called it "inwardness."

Stendhal and Nietzsche understood the nature and fate of the exceptional man who is surrounded by mediocrity. Kierkegaard and Dostoevsky, on the contrary, were preoccupied with the destiny of man without God. One way to appreciate this division is to observe the different attitudes toward passion which Stendhal and Kierkegaard take. Both speak of passion as something that the middle-class lacks. To the former, passion is the outsider's style; to the latter it is only a symptom of inwardness. To the former, passion serves to distinguish; to the latter it makes sure that an individual does not look at himself as an object. A Stendhalian hero is marvelously alert to everything and everyone around him; Kierkegaard with a Pascalian passion seeks eternal happiness. We think of Stendhal and his characters as strangers in their own time because they show the two basic features of a new kind of isolation: a contempt for insensitivity and a pursuit of art and love. They are distinguished from Dostoevsky and his characters by their almost complete objec-

19

tivity toward ..hemselves. They are constantly, childishly, frivolously amazed at themselves, curious about what will happen next, reminiscent over what has already occurred. They show a detachment from themselves which would be unthinkable in a novel by Dostoevsky.

In Stendhal self-dissection is developed to a very high degree, but he is no more self-analytical than Kierkegaard. In fact, Kierkegaard's interior life was lived at a level of which Stendhal was almost ignorant. A person who has his mind primarily on the relation between himself and his environment is not likely to think about "boundary situations" (Karl Jaspers), but rather on his own talents, aspirations, and failures. Stendhal and his heroes and heroines are restless, but only because they feel hemmed in by an unsympathetic society. A man who does not know the meaning of "inwardness" is obsessed by time in a different way. He may lament having lost or wasted time, and of having little time left, but only because he had missed opportunities, not because he had not yet found God.

There is only a page or so by Stendhal where he shows any awareness of the possibility of "inwardness," but it is very moving passage at that. It is at the end of *The Red and the Black* where Julien Sorel, in prison and condemned to death, unable to think of life any longer as a pursuit of glory, unable also to anticipate life with either lady he loves, speculates in a mood of depression on what is gone and what might be. With his mind darting desperately back and forth between longing and disillusion he says,

> There is no such thing as natural law . . . there is nothing natural save the strength of the lion . . . . Everywhere hypocrisy . . . . Man cannot place any trust in man . . . . Where is truth? . . . Ah! if there were a true religion, a true priest . . . . Then the tender hearts would have a meeting-place in this world . . . . We would not remain isolated. . . . How is one to believe in that great name of God, after the frightful abuse that our priests make of it? . . . To live in isolation! . . . What torture! . . . The influence of my contemporaries is too strong for me. . . . Talking alone to myself within an inch of death, I am still a hypocrite . . . . Oh, nineteenth century!

At this place only did Stendhal conceive in his writing a religious measure of man. He goes on to describe Julien imagining a hunter and some ants (cf. a similar passage in Hemingway's *Farewell to Arms*). The hunter has fired his gun and rushed forward to pick up his victim; in doing so he steps on an anthill. "The most philosophical among the ants will never understand that black, enormous, fearful body . . . . So it is with death, life, eternity, things that would be quite simple to anyone who had organs vast enough to conceive them." The fly born in the morning, dying in the evening, if it lived a few hours longer it would understand what night is. Man too would understand if he had organs vast enough. But this is a momentary wonderment born of a despair which the author swiftly puts in its proper perspective. "Alas! Madame de Renal is absent . . . . That is what is isolating me, that and not the absence of a just, good, all-powerful God." But even if such a God existed, "I should fall at his feet, I should say to him, but great God, good God, indulgent God, restore to me her whom I love."

Compare this with Dostoevsky's recurrent questions: "Do you know what it means to be alone? . . . Do you understand, sir, what it means to have absolutely nowhere to turn?" These are the questions of one who has no hope and cannot even say, "*If* I had so and so, everything would be as it should be." Inwardness is not to be defined by its external setting, such as solitude or failure, but by the innate capacity of an individual to see the difference between his fate as an individual and his fate as a human. Dostoevsky's characters are cut off from their environment more completely than Stendhal's, but they do not think in terms of environment, and that is why they always ask the eternal questions about love, God, immortality, and suffering. It is as if Stendhal were to say, "Give me the woman I love, and I won't care about questions and answers." And it is as if Dostoevsky were saying, "Give me an ultimate answer so that I may live." Much later Kafka wrote of "a young man who thought of nothing but the Castle day and night, he neglected everything else, and people feared for his reason, his mind was so wholly absorbed by the Castle. It turned out at length, however, that it wasn't really the Castle he was thinking of, but the daughter of a charwoman in the offices up there, so he got the girl and was all right again."

When we pass from Stendhal to Dostoevsky, we pass from a world of successes and fiascos to a world of longing and despair. And the middle ground is occupied by Kierkegaard's recovery of inwardness. Stendhal did not need a new word for his own relationship to opportunities and talents. Only because Kierkegaard was trying to define what he called "the God-relationship" in man, was a new word needed. "My principal thought was that in our age because of the great increase of knowledge, we had forgotten what it means to exist, what inwardness signifies, and that the misunderstanding between speculative philosophy and Christianity was explicable on that ground." In *The Concept of Dread* he had already said that "if inwardness is lacking, the spirit is finitized . . . . Inwardness is therefore eternity, or the determinant of the eternal in a man." He was often to complain that people were so admiring of science and encyclopedic knowledge that they no longer thought of suffering, sin, and death. "What the age needs is an awakening."

He who had dedicated books to "the revival and increase of inwardness" argued that one could not know what it is to be a Christian if he did not know what it is to exist, and that he could not know what it is to exist unless he knew inwardness. Unfortunately, inwardness was a term that even Bishop Mynster used. The Bishop had said that you could not tell a Christian from his words, that he might have a "hidden inwardness." Kierkegaard for a while enjoyed imagining that he too was a "knight of the hidden inwardness"—until he realized that such a distinction would make it possible for anyone else to pretend the same apostolic fervor, without cost. And so he came more and more to believe that no one is a Christian who has not "suffered for the doctrine." Although later abandoning the phrase "hidden inwardness," he never abandoned his effort to differentiate between the intense religious awareness he had of his existence, and the duller awareness of life that other men seemed to get along with. To him inwardness was a consciousness of a tension within the soul requiring some decision involving a change

of life, what Karl Jaspers, borrowing from Kierkegaard, called existential boundary situations. Even an aesthete could feel such a tension and make up his mind to reshape his life.

Stendhalian tension is either wholly internal, head *vs.* heart, or
external, individual *vs.* society. His heroes are never put on trial
because they are human, but only because they do not fit in. No
decision binds forever, no judgment from without is authoritative,
unless backed up by police. Kierkegaardian tension is, as he aptly
called it, a "sickness unto death"; it can be repressed but not cured.
It is made up of a divine imperative, as the command of God to
Abraham, demanding obedience. And it is experienced in the subconscious as depression, and in the conscience as guilt or sin, the
knowledge of God's magnetism and man's slowness to respond. When
an individual experiences God's overwhelming care for him,
man is "always in the wrong." For how can he measure up to the
infinite concern, how can he place his own life infinitely and passionately in God's hands? And because he feels this is what is
required of him, he feels he is being asked to do the impossible. No
wider gulf separates man than that which gapes between him and the
eternal.

Compare this sense of internal paradox with Stendhal's inner and
outer conflicts. Had Kierkegaard read Stendhal, he would probably
have said of him too, "He isn't serious." He himself spoke of two
opposing ways of looking at reality, either as ideas, approximations
of truth, or as an existential whole. So he wished to distinguish
between the incompleteness of science and philosophy on the one
hand, and the moral transformation that is demanded by an acceptance of the God-relationship in human life. This relationship, he
claimed, man can know absolutely, and only this absolutely. But it
is something a person can know only of and in himself; he cannot
know for sure the state of any other person's inwardness. This is
why Kierkegaard always talked of inwardness as "subjectivity"
and "certitude." It is the only certitude a man can achieve, the
truth of his own existence. It is the one certitude the nineteenth
century lacked. But it is a certitude which seems to reduce the heroic
stature of man, and therefore something a proud man may reject.

Stendhalian self-consciousness enlarges the hero, makes him feel important. Kierkegaardian inwardness is the awareness of his smallness, his human frailty. There is no certitude more unassailable than when the self knows itself as contingent or sinful, when it encounters something as absolutely different as the ever-living God, or when it is so sunk in its guilt that it yearns for deliverance. In Dostoevsky's novels the God-seekers look for human love as well. But Kierkegaard had become so imprisoned in his melancholy, "my castle," that he could not believe in human love as a solution. He who had tried to become "contemporaneous" with the Christ could not believe he could become contemporaneous with Regine Olsen. Perhaps he could not because he had so much difficulty becoming contemporaneous with a God ready to forgive even a Kierkegaard who was not ready to accept forgiveness.

THE MARGINS OF SOLITUDE

Dostoevsky never had to think of inwardness as such a new experience that a special term was needed for it. He wrote from within a more metaphysically turbulent scene, and many of his Russian contemporaries knew well the same inner tensions known to Kierkegaard alone. To modern ears there may be something unscientific in Kierkegaard's insistence that inwardness be understood as subjectivity. He had chosen this word aggressively as the way calculated to mark off two antithetical ways an individual can take to see himself. The objective knower is impartial, and therefore to be trusted; the subjective knower knows only himself, and cannot be trusted to say anything of universal significance. Kierkegaard would have admitted this, and yet he felt that subjectivity or inwardness was a lost habit which it was his mission to restore. He saw a connection between inwardness and Socratic dialectic, for Socrates too had pursued truth for the sake of personal edification, knowledge for the sake of virtue, truth for the sake of an idea that a man can live by. And for Socrates also man must ultimately be understood in terms of a God-relationship, to Law, Justice, the Good. But Kierkegaard seemed

not to have noticed that Socrates, unlike himself, was not passionately, infinitely interested in his own Socratic happiness. This helps
to explain the absence of tension in Socrates at and after his trial.

If inwardness is metaphysical tension within the soul, it is clearly
not original with Kierkegaard. He was, however, the first to speak
in philosophical language of the scope of this tension. In a religious
age there would be no other conscience to differentiate it from;
everyone would know inwardness. It is not a coincidence, therefore,
that the man who discovered "inwardness" as a philosophical category should feel it was his "Socratic task to revise the definition of
what it is to be a Christian," "to reintroduce Christianity into Christendom." He disclaimed being an example or an apostle—"I am
without authority, I do not call myself a Christian." "My task is to
make room that God may come." His posthumous authority has
been truly enormous, and others have felt justified in calling him
Christian and apostle.

While the comparison with Socrates breaks down at a certain
point, the comparison with Pascal suggests a more profound as well
as a wider context than even Kierkegaard, who "loved" Pascal, knew.
Pascal's underlying theme is the Augustinian disquietude; such is
the condition of man. But St. Augustine believed that men are restless because they have wandered from the God of their hearts, and
Pascal saw the source of disquietude in man's fear of cosmic homelessness. "The infinite spaces frighten me." He saw another cause
too, the frustration of not being able to know the God one already
loves. "We are incapable of knowing either what God is or whether
he exists." To turn away the fear, men divert and distract, inventing
business and games and complacency. Thus they avoid seeing their
true position in the universe or the risks in attaining eternal life.
Men may be miserable without God, if they know it, but they are
more likely to be aware of their forlornness as microcosms in an
indifferent universe.

So man lives either in the past or in the future, remembering or
anticipating, always avoiding the present that he is really made for,
and from which he has fallen. Disquietude is the built-in memory of
the pain after the fall. Only in a fallen state would man be oppressed

by the infinite in any form, and not rather be reminded of the glory and grandeur of the infinite God. Disquietude is the mark and the symptom of a creature unable to live up to the promise of eternity built in itself. Man living alone in a neutral universe, imagines himself under sentence of death. "Let us imagine a number of men in chains, and all condemned to death, where some are killed each day in the sight of others, and those who remain see their own fate in their fellows, and wait their turn, looking at each other sorrowfully and without hope. It is an image of the condition of man." It is not, however, St. Augustine's image. It is Kierkegaard's, Dostoevsky's (and—with a difference—Plato's).

St. Augustine's image is of two cities, one which is founded on the love of God, the other on love of self. The image is social, embracing the conception of a home to which man can go back. God is not a familiar of Pascal or Kierkegaard, but as remote as for Isaiah or Jeremiah. He is far away—except as Hemingway would say, "sometimes at night." If he does not come in the night, man must take a chance, wager, leap into his presence, catch him by surprise (as Kafka would catch the officials of the Castle). Most of the time the human condition as understood by Pascal and Kierkegaard is simply and depressingly a "being unto death" (Heidegger). If man has any hope, it must be directed to the charity which God has offered through his Son and which some buried memory of man's greatness may yet respond to.

Kierkegaard's solitude, on the other hand, is the solitude of the single one who knows he is a sinner, and who is doubly lonely because he knows inwardness while others do not. Those whom Pascal so scornfully accused of wasting time which should be used in seeking God, the freethinkers of the seventeenth century, lived side by side with some of the most God-loving individuals Christendom has known. Whenever a phoney Christianity satisfies church-goers, there are no sheep because there is no fold; there are, to use the Kierkegaardian comic image, only wild geese and tame geese. The wild geese do not remember ever having been tame geese; but they may yet enjoy that fate. In the meantime they do not, so to speak, honk the same language. So Kierkegaard himself had to learn to speak two languages, one for aesthetic man, the other for ethical and religious man. Pascal, on the other hand, spoke to freethinkers as he spoke to himself, the language of the enlightenment. And unlike Kierkegaard he associated normally with men and women of sympathetic religious persuasion at Port Royal. Kierkegaard's exacerbated sense of the difference between himself and everyone about him—as violent as Nietzsche's—made it natural that he should think of his dilemmas as universal problems that he alone had re-discovered.

Perhaps he was the first to explain them, even if he was not the first to experience them. By the nineteenth century Protestant Christians (the only ones Kierkegaard knew) had so diluted Christianity that they could not have appreciated the turbulence of Jansenism or of Pascal. This is why almost everything Kierkegaard wrote was spoiled by his exasperation with the time in which he lived. Not nearly so preoccupied as Pascal with man's loneliness in the macrocosm, not nearly so obsessed by his inherited sense of sin as he himself thought, Kierkegaard let himself be bogged down in an unedifying bickering with the Copenhagen bourgeoisie.

Because inwardness is consciousness of a certain kind of tension, it can be spoken of both as subjectivity, introspection, and as a dynamic encounter between finite and infinite. And this is what Kierkegaard does. One moment he is stressing the introspection, and a little further on he is making much of the despairing, guilty character of the encounter. Sometimes we hear so loudly his insistence to his complacently extroverted contemporaries that "subjectivity is the truth," or "becoming subjective is the task proposed to every human being," that we forget what it is all about. To be subjective is, for Kierkegaard, ultimately to be aware that "as against God we are always in the wrong."

There is yet another aspect of subjectivity which Kierkegaard did not go into, but which we can see in Dostoevsky's novels: "Do you know what it means to be alone?" And Kierkegaard would have replied, "If I do not, who does?" Had not the young S.K. imagined himself a lonely pine tree egoistically shut off, pointing to the skies and casting no shadow, and only the turtle-dove builds its nest in my branches. I am in the profoundest sense an unhappy individuality which from its earliest years has been nailed fast to some suffering or other bordering upon madness. . . . I feel so foreign to, so different from everything that normally occupies people—continually surrounded by curiosity, always a stranger, now envied, now ridiculed, now admired, now coarsely gaped at.

He was an outsider indeed, from birth and choice. And he knew as well the Pascalian cosmic homelessness in its literal form. "The whole of existence frightens me, from the smallest fly to the mystery of the Incarnation; everything is unintelligible to me, most of all myself; the whole of existence is poisoned in my sight, particularly myself."

If Kierkegaardian inwardness is not just a new word for a vaguely interior life, but rather a way of bringing up the question of God, it is plain that inwardness is utterly unlike Stendhalian self-analysis (which is what most people still mean by introspection). Dostoevsky's heroes and heroines are similarly concerned with the question of God; he, however, explains the search and the tension in one way, Kierkegaard in another. May the difference be simply that for Kierkegaard the tension always represents a conflict between the creature and the fearful judgment of the Creator, between guilt and passion? And that for the tragic Stavroguin or Underground Man there can be no longing at all? This may be, and yet even these figures recognize the misery of their self-isolation, and Stavroguin at least knows he is miserable without God. Moreover, other Dostoevsky characters do yearn for an infinite being in whom they do not yet believe but who represents the binding life force in all things.

This does not do complete justice to Kierkegaard. For when he speaks of his hope of introducing inwardness in the life of an aesthetic man, he means that he would like the aesthete to see life as a tension between an instinct for happiness and the impossibility already demonstrated by life and luck of being happy as long as he looks for everything to come from outside. Whoever can understand this tension does think inwardly, Socratically, but he is not thinking

Christianly. Man is always on trial; they would agree. In the transition between the aesthetic and the ethical, the judge is interior man himself, as he sentences himself for failing to measure up to the universal requirements of a human being. But in the hoped-for transition between the ethical and the religious, the individual no longer judges but is judged by God, and against him man is always in the wrong. Socrates had no experience of a judgment that absolute. Nor did he know the Christian way to live with that judgment without despair.

We must say that Kierkegaard was using himself as an example for his theology. His introspection at the crossroads of faith was very troubled. He had been a seducer and had written a definitive word about seduction. He had been a romantic who understood the despair in the aesthetic's thin soul. He had taken back his word to a trusting girl, and yet demanded that other men live by law. He knew that a normal man should marry and work; he did neither. He passionately believed in forgiveness, but would not submit to the forgiveness he himself needed and desired. Did he fear that forgiveness accepted would release love?

He had prescribed Socratic inwardness as a preparation for religious inwardness. A man must know himself before he can hear the call to Christ. If only he has passion enough, he will choose the right course, for passion is the intensification of the divine-human encounter to the point where the self knows the poles of the tension and the alternatives extended. If he knows the terms, he will know one as higher than the other, the ethical higher than the aesthetic, the religious higher than the ethical. But will he necessarily choose the higher? Socrates said yes, and Kierkegaard wanted to agree. And yet he himself had clung to his melancholy. He said, of course, that he had chosen the higher ground, God's, but he himself was never wholly sure. "If I had had the strength, I would have married her." What God was to him, as the great smasher-in of self-isolation, God was to Dostoevsky as the one near whom there might be no will to power. Dostoevsky's heroes never get to a place where their reason can accept what their hearts long for. For that matter, Dostoevsky did not think that men ever break loose from self-will after they have chosen God, but rather, if they are to at all, before. Like St. Augustine, St. Anselm, and Pascal, Dostoevsky too was convinced that we believe in order to understand.

THE QUESTION OF THE SUFFERER

To be subjective is to be subjected, not only to the authority of infinite over finite, but to the self-love of the finite. Kierkegaard's introspection has both aspects. But in Dostoevsky's novels they are separated, handed over to different sorts of heroes: those who know the agony of self-enclosure, and those who are miserable without God. Even here there is a difference. Not only is Stavroguin to be distinguished from Ivan by this; Ivan is opposed to Kierkegaard, as a person who cannot believe in God but would like to is to be distinguished from one who believes with his whole heart and soul. The spirit broods more glowingly in Dostoevsky's characters just because they are so troubled by their inability to be free of themselves. Stavroguin and Ivan cannot give themselves in love, and yet Stavroguin is free enough to do evil and Ivan to permit it. Both know what they do, and love and hate simultaneously. Their wills are in bondage and they suffer.

There may be worse ways of suffering, but this curious ambivalence of the will is open to some men who cannot suffer in any other way. Ivan Karamazov instinctively realizes this, and that is why he talks so much about the suffering of children. He says he loves the children, whom he does not see, but cannot love the grown-ups, whom he does see. He can tell us more about the nature of man than Stavroguin and yet is more inhibited than Stavroguin.

Kierkegaard said that whoever suffers for the doctrine also dies to the world and is, as a result, raised above his fellows in lonely honor. Dostoevsky was equally sure that whoever suffers from paralysis of will is also separated from other men; he will die. "And except a corn of wheat fall into the ground and die, it abideth alone; but if it die, it bringeth forth much fruit" (St. John). Nietzsche, who suffered from non-recognition, and from bodily illnesses as well, knew a great deal about "the discipline of suffering," but it was a discipline that encouraged him to think that "profound suffering makes noble, it separates." This is not why Lise in *The Brothers Karamazov* wanted to suffer. She longed to descend to the level of real suffering of the poor, so that she herself could atone for her comfort, her frivolity, and her innocence. She jammed her finger in a door; she scolded Alyosha. And of her he said, that her sympathy for the destitute Snegiryovs showed "the question of a sufferer." She had wanted to reach this point of being taken seriously, and of carrying a corner of someone else's burden.

How different from Nietzsche who always recoiled—or was he overacting—from the everyday suffering of others, because he thought people should not be encouraged to be sorry for themselves, but rather to make the most of their inborn will to power. We remember that he also thought suffering at best could be "the anguish of fullness and overfullness, the suffering of the contradictions concentrated within." But he meant by this the creative birth pangs which come not only from undeveloped and disordered strivings but from the magnitude of energy and the microscopic size of its outlet.

His Dionysian suffering was not, of course, the same as the frustration of not being recognized by contemporaries, and not the same as the migraines and intestinal cramps from which he almost constantly suffered. And perhaps he did not know himself as thoroughly as he supposed when he boasted that he had rejected ordinary suffering because he did not want to encourage others to surrender before the fight. He was a snob about suffering: otherwise why should be think non-recognition any better or worse a suffering than cancer or losing a job or a wife? Probably he knew—and feared—that whoever is sorry for someone else cannot sustain his isolation. He would have us believe that "egoism belongs to the essence of a noble soul," and that through egoism he himself was avoiding "the European disease—the sickness of the will." Before he was through, he himself experienced more than one sickness of the will.

Kierkegaard, Dostoevsky, and Nietzsche all plead for readers who will understand them and "accept suffering." Kierkegaard too showed little interest in non-artistic, non-metaphysical agonies. How warmly, however, he could sympathize with the anguish of a man isolated by sin or doctrine, namely a man like himself. Dostoevsky, on the other hand, believed that by accepting suffering a man may stop judging others from the easy distance of self-concern. Then the mutual responsibility of mankind will appear. The torment of Ivan and Stavroguin discharges the secret tensions of inwardness, and Dostoevsky's novels are kept moving not only by the promise of disclosure of some unknown future, but by the hope of learning some secret of character as well. The reader learns the secret which the hero holds within him at the moment the hero confesses to someone else. And when it is passed on to another person, Alyosha, for example, he in turn accepts the secret and stores it up as a privileged burden.

CONTEMPORANEOUSNESS AND SILENCE

Kierkegaard defined the proper relationship between an individual and Christ as "contemporaneousness" (like so much of his terminology, clumsily abstract). "The absolute has no existence for him who is not contemporary with it. . . . As Christ is the absolute, with respect to Him there is only one situation, that of contemporaneousness. . . . A believer must be just as contemporary with His presence on earth as were those contemporaries." Kierkegaard probably had never read St. Leo's maxim that the same power is to be found in Church and sacraments as in the historical Christ. But he knew the temptation to assume that a man who has been dead for eighteen hundred years can hardly seem very present now. Nowhere does Kierkegaard make the orthodox Catholic distinction between the crucified man and the new Christ in the Church, the continuation of the Incarnation in its new body. The thrust of his own theology was ethical, as he exhorted men to be followers rather than admirers, first renouncing the world, the flesh, and the devil. From then on the convert should anticipate suffering for the doctrine. But "buried with Christ in his death and also partaker of his resurrection" (*The Book of Common Prayer*), he will have a good reason to accept suffering.

This is not very different from Zossima's injunction to accept suffering so that men may become brothers to each other. Kierkegaard hoped that through renunciation of world and self-will, men could become brothers to Christ. But he also felt sure that a follower of Christ would feel cut off from most men—and women—or else with an uneasy conscience would begin to doubt his discipleship. Kierkegaard was barely interested in the cries of innocent victims. And yet he always believed with all his heart that the way to become at one with Christ is the way of inwardness, of self brooding away on God's command to love and be forgiven. He said that the soul on trial before God must first decide for or against God, and if for God then against self and the world. But once under judgment and aware of a world in agony, he must also decide for or against his own self-concern, and then must sacrificially carry the cross for the world.

This act of atonement can only be made in silence, that prime "condition of inwardness, of the inner life." "The first thing to be done is to introduce silence, God's word cannot be heard." Nervousness and restlessness are so distracting, the disquietudes of inwardness are so self-contained and concentrated, that the self is compelled to come to terms with the poles of tension where, in the silence of its conscience, its fate can be decided. "It was one of those moments," says Dostoevsky, "which come perhaps to everyone, but only once in a lifetime. At such moments men decide their fate, define their point of view, and say to themselves once and forever where the truth lies." Only in silence can a perfect judgment be rendered, and only when the self is fully present to itself, collected after its weary wanderings. To belong to Christ, to stand by others when they suffer, you must first accept yourself. Silence is the prerequisite for being present to oneself, which in turn is the preparation for being present to others. In this sense also Stendhal's self-analysis is a world apart from the interior life of Kierkegaard and Dostoevsky; it has no silence in it. Stendhal is always playing with his toys.

THE TRUTH THAT CHANGES

In inwardness man meets God, but not as equals meet, as head meets heart, but as unequals, finite with infinite. In misery and in longing the characteristic resonances of inwardness play their poignant tunes, signifying the tension between incompatibles. This is as true for Pascal as for Kierkegaard and Dostoevsky, who, seeing that the universe and man, reason and truth, are incompatible, the human situation forlorn, urged his readers to stake all on an Infinite Chance, the God of Charity. For Kierkegaard the incompatibility is moral rather than rational; God is perfect, man hopelessly imperfect. To make matters worse, reason cannot comprehend the God-man paradox. And so some men forget inwardness altogether—which means they forget their eternal destiny—unless they are daring enough to throw themselves on God's mercy. In turn, Dostoevsky held that man shut up in himself longs for the corporate redemption that love should be able to provide, but which most men do not know how to give or receive gracefully. When Kierkegaard speaks of inwardness as subjectivity, as the conscience of a subject who is opposed by men who think objectively, and who call their subjectivity a sickness, he is thinking of two radically different truths: the abstract truth which the inquiring mind edges ever closer to—and which assumes an absolute distance between knower and known—and the personal truth which can change a man's life.

Dostoevsky's inwardness takes the form of brooding, and so superficially differs from that of Pascal or Kierkegaard. And in fact, Dostoevsky's characters hardly ever come to the point of final commitment. Although Kierkegaard could not break out of his own self-isolation completely, he had no trouble deciding whether he should, or whether God exists. Pascal too had no trouble in believing in God. Both he and Kierkegaard had experienced the presence of God first-hand. "Fire . . . God of Abraham, God of Isaac, God of Jacob, not of the philosophers and savants . . . Certitude . . . Certitude . . .

Feeling . . . Joy . . . Peace . . . God of Jesus Christ" (Pascal's "Memorial"). "My whole being is changed. My reserve and self-isolation is broken—I must speak . . . Lord give thy grace" (Kierkegaard's journal entry, April 19, 1848). Dostoevsky, on the other hand, claiming no personal mystical experiences persisted throughout his writings to ask whether there is a God at all. Perhaps because of the fact that from childhood he had an intimate penitential relationship with God which insulated him against fundamental religious skepticism, it was much easier for Kierkegaard to believe in God than it was for Dostoevsky. The tragedy of Kierkegaard's inwardness was justified—in the religious sense, made right—to some extent by his real faith. But even on his deathbed he had not completely resolved the tension between this faith and his self-isolation. Dostoevsky was never inwardly sure that doubt could be vanquished by faith.

Through faith Kierkegaard accepted the tension in which man is delivered to judgment, and in accepting the sentence that against God we are always in the wrong, he reached the stage where the only question left was the offensiveness of his own stubborn self-isolation. If that could be broken, tension would be lifted altogether and he would then live at peace with himself. No such halfway success was achieved by most of Dostoevsky's characters who could not believe in God no matter how much they loved the image of Christ. The more they agonized over their unbelief and numbness of will, the more universal they took their own dilemmas to be. This is why Ivan Karamazov insists that without a belief in God and immortality there is no natural law to love, only self-will.

The outsider experiences in inwardness an intimacy—for this is what contemporaneousness means—which his age could not give him. Or at least he learned that he must live under a suspended sentence, until he could resolve the tension between himself and God. Is it not ironic that the outsider who wished to put his contemporaries on trial should end by finding himself on trial instead? What makes his ordeal even more interesting to us is that he was not arrested because he failed to get along as an outsider, but because he had within him an instinct for eternity which tore him apart.

CHAPTER 4

Excursion into Chaos

"Two extremes, gentlemen of the jury, remember that Karamazov can contemplate two extremes and both at once."—Dostoevsky

THE MAN WHO "knows inwardness" feels that he ought to be able to break out of his self-will by loving or by believing. But he may not be able to move to a clear decision in favor of another person or of God. If he does not, he then represses inwardness and his journey into isolation terminates. But if he is fortunate enough to be released, then he may never come to experience the demonic horrors of moral doubleness. Kierkegaard's faith did not exclude self-isolation, but it was a safeguard against doubleness. He who is open to the reality of either divine or human love, does not need to fall back on the ambiguities of Dostoevskian diabolism. And he whose consciousness of the power of love is repressed, needs to substitute some other goal for which he can strive. Moral doubleness or diabolism is a substitute for the power and reality of some kind of love.

Inwardness does not distinguish, as the moral conscience does, between right and wrong, but only between finite and infinite. It is a measure of the finite, the high trial of the finite, asking the finite to accept the judgment of the infinite. If the finite accepts, the inwardness of the individual is on the way to fulfilling itself and the individual. Kierkegaard understood inwardness in this way, and was himself on the road to self-fulfillment before he became frustrated in his self-isolation. He remains an enigma because of some dark, obstinate secret of his makeup. Only one of Dostoevsky's famous characters, Raskolnikov, was permitted by that author to complete his inward course and break through into the open. The rest were tormented by repressed longing, real love and life being denied them

36

and belief in God withheld. In some the awareness of the reasons for their brooding was just plain enough for them to feel close to breaking away from the chains of their inner tension; in others the tension was not understood on a high enough plane for them even to feel the mystery of their repression.

It is important to acknowledge that the doubles are repressed persons suffering from frustrations which Dostoevsky progressively refined as he advanced through his novels. And one cannot deny that most of these characters exhibit symptoms which are easily labelled pathological. One is schizophrenic, several are epileptic, some suffer from hallucinations, all have strange dreams, some collapse from "brain fever," some kill themselves. Most show signs of sadism and masochism. Whatever the psychiatric diagnosis of Dostoevsky himself, his readers can in all fairness be concerned only with the diagnoses he himself has given in his novels.

Whoever moves on from reading Stendhal to reading Kierkegaard and Dostoevsky senses that he is in new territory, metaphysical or religious. He may express this change very simply by conceding that there is no guilt in Stendhal. Nor is there any repression either, except on the political level, and that is forced on the outsider who makes a nuisance of himself. But there is spontaneity, and a good deal of calculated self-control. And yet a Stendhalian character, however spontaneous or calculating, is innocent and pure of heart compared to a Stavroguin or Svidrigailov. He loves some things, places, ideals, persons, and hates others, but he never hates that which he loves, unless he hates someone who has snubbed him.

Kierkegaard too was able to alternate between his self-isolation and God's forgiveness and love. He never doubted the human mind's ability to make the right choice; had not he himself made it? The only question left was whether he could so break out of his self-isolation that he might become an apostle acting solely on call from God. Dostoevsky, on the other hand, did doubt the mind's capability of making the right decision; he thought man as well as his age was sick. Only the sick man, neurotically or morally sick, feels attracted to evil. The only superiority of Stendhal to the other three is that he did not have this sickness. For one thing, he had little sense of any evil that was not social or political. In this he was bourgeois, completely adjusted to a view of life in which no misfortune is unmanageable. In fact, by the bourgeois evil is regarded not as crime but as bad luck.

Misfortune is certainly not attractive, and it is unthinkable that anyone should be attracted to it. Kierkegaard, however, knew the attractiveness of evil in the involuntary experiences of the demoniacal and original sin. But he himself did not go out of his way to be sinful. Unlike Dostoevsky he could not think of life in terms of "the life of a great sinner," but only in terms of the unexceptional sinning of original sin. He did not think that a great passion need lead to great sin. "Even if a man were to choose the wrong, he will nevertheless discover, precisely by reason of the energy with which he chose, that he had chosen the wrong. For the choice being made with the whole inwardness of his personality, his nature is purified and he himself brought into immediate relation to the Eternal Power whose omnipresence interpenetrates the whole of existence." Such a view is possible, of course, only to one who has no doubt that God's omnipresence does interpenetrate the whole of existence. Otherwise, passion and energy might flow just as surely to "the wrong." Kierkegaard could not conceive choosing evil on purpose, and he did not fear that a man might choose evil by mistake either. For him Goodness and Mercy are always near. The problem is whether to give oneself to God or hold back.

Doubleness is not a Kierkegaardian category, for doubleness is a certain response an individual makes when his inwardness is repressed, and Kierkegaard had no first-hand experience of doubleness to draw on for his theory about the demoniacal. He knew much about despair, but because he himself never lost faith, he did not know the issue that despair takes when it lives without hope.

THE AMBIVALENCE OF LOVE AND HATE

If it is better to trust God or another human being rather than hurt someone in order to prove one's independence, it is better also to brandish good alone and not good and evil simultaneously. For simultaneous postulation of good and evil is a sign of a will that cannot make up its mind, and takes no chances of being right or wrong. Stavroguin says, "I am still capable as I always was, of desiring to do something good and of feeling pleasure from it; at the same time I desire evil and feel pleasure from that too." It is the "at the same time" that distinguishes Stavroguin from a genuinely free man. This is a nice way of talking about repression, or "unfreedom" (Kierkegaard), and the moral ambivalence of Stavroguin has its affective counterpart. How often someone in one of the stories says, "You may be in love with a woman and yet hate her." "Behind the love she feels for me . . . which is sincere too, every moment there are flashes of hatred . . . the most intense hatred." This is not a question of real hatred and unreal love, but of a love just as real as the hate. "Karamazov can contemplate two extremes and both at once."

Is this true of everyone or just of "doubles"? Baudelaire said, "There are in every man at every moment two simultaneous postulations, one towards God, the other towards Satan." And some men —perhaps even Baudelaire—are interested in neither God nor Satan, but only in themselves. Ivan Karamazov insisted that "everyone hates his father." Must one believe this "everyone"? All doubles have some simultaneity, but is it true that all men are doubles? Or is it even true that all men could be doubles? Stendhal hated his father, and Stendhal was no double. Could he have been a double? What does such a question mean? All that we know is that some men act as doubles and some do not. Some exhibit moral and affective ambivalence, and some do not. Those who do, may also be schizophrenic, with no control over their ambivalence. But if they have some control over their caprice, we can assume that they act capriciously as a conscious way out of a dilemma which may not be otherwise clear to them. The double in Dostoevsky's novels lives out such a dilemma.

We should want to know also whether a man whose inwardness is repressed must show the ambivalences of love and hate, good and evil. Could he substitute another ambivalence for the ambivalence of caprice? Could he postulate, for example, as Raskolnikov does, a simultaneity of reason and pity? Or would that be an expression of inwardness rather than repressed inwardness? There is little doubt that within both Ivan and Raskolnikov reason and pity exist, side by side in Ivan, and on different levels in Raskolnikov. And there is no doubt that just as Raskolnikov represses pity boldly, Ivan's interest in God cannot, for some reason, get beyond the stage of the hypothetical. In this sense one could say that he does not accept the judgment of infinite compassion over his reason, because his belief in the infinite is repressed by his reason. Repressed on this level, he allows his pity for humanity to run riot in fancifulness.

There is a progression in Dostoevsky's own understanding of the double, from his early story "The Double" through *The Brothers Karamazov*. He may have been trying to explain something about himself. It may well be that his final explanations are not real ones, but only the ones which relieved him of the greatest humiliation. Nevertheless, it is plausible that a man whose very awareness of the terms of inwardness is repressed, may seek in the simultaneities of the double, substitutes for right acts. Caprice may look free to a man who holds that freedom is present only when one can do evil as well as good, and must do evil in order to prove it. But caprice looks unfree to a man who does not wish to be condemned to a perpetual shuttling between the desire to be free and a proof of freedom that requires evil. We may be independent of others when we hurt them, but no one is free who feels he has to do evil in order to know that he is independent. Whoever will do evil for such a reason suffers from repressed inwardness. This takes two forms: where inwardness is trying to break into the open and is being held back, and where it is in the open already and cannot come to a decision. In both cases a man may resort to doubleness of one sort or another as a way out of a trap.

"The Double" is interesting now mainly because it was Dostoevsky's first attempt to describe repression. He wrote it three years before he was sent to Siberia. It is long-winded, and Dostoevsky soon knew enough about repression not to be satisfied with its unrealistic simplification. It is a story of pathological schizophrenia, and seems to have little or no moral significance. The main character, Mr. Golyadkin, is a so-called titular councilor in some Petersburg section of the civil service, an unimportant official doing some undefined paper-pushing. He would like to be envied by colleagues, and loved by the daughter of the boss. He is neither envied nor loved, and makes a fool of himself one day when he masquerades on borrowed money as a wealthy playboy. Humiliated by the disrespect of everyone he tries to impress, he begins to see his double, another Mr. Golyadkin, working in the same office, prospering as the real Mr. Golyadkin declines. In the end "our hero," as Dostoevsky tiresomely calls him, is removed to the madhouse.

Although Mr. Golyadkin is obviously suffering from the many frustrations of a small man in a big city, neither he nor his maker makes this explicit. His schizophrenia is certainly involuntary. When he consults a doctor, he is told to change his habits but not his habitat. "Entertainment, for instance, and friends—you should visit your acquaintances and not be hostile to the bottle . . . likewise keep cheerful company." The prescription is useless because the diagnosis has missed the mark. Dostoevsky's "double" is an early figure of anonymous urban man, no roots, no home, no job worth doing. Looked at from the outside he is both comic and pathetic by turns, and neither the author nor the reader is tempted to identify himself with his bewilderment. Never again did Dostoevsky write of an hallucinatory double.

When he next took up the problem of repressed personality, after returning from his prison experiences in Siberia, he described (in *Notes from Underground*) the life of another anonymous man who not only does have some idea of the meaning of his predicament but who uses affective and moral ambivalence as a way out. "The Double" is told in the third person; *Notes from Underground* is told in the first. The Underground Man does not have a proper name; he could be anyone living in the same circumstances. In fact, the author insists in a note, the Underground Man "not only may but positively must exist in our society, when we consider the circumstances in the midst of which our society is formed . . . . He is one of the representatives of a generation still living." These "notes" are autobiographical in tone, and the reader gets involved in the emotions of the narrator without intending to, they are so embarrassingly uninhibited.

The Underground Man is also a civil servant, a bachelor without friends. He was practically an orphan, and treated badly at school. He too is tiresomely garrulous, and yet timid in public, a dreamer rather than a doer. But he has a habit of humiliating himself before others in order to be noticed. He is the first of Dostoevsky's many buffoons. He is not necessarily psychotic, however much his behavior imitates the symptoms of schizophrenia. From beginning to end he knows what he is doing. He speaks of himself as sick from the inertia and over-consciousness of his time, and yet we wonder why spite should be particularly symptomatic of that sickness and that time. Why not the opposite, depression?

The Underground Man does not, unlike Mr. Golyadkin, bother with doctors; he already knows what is ailing him and knows there is no cure. Spite keeps him going. Because no one thing or person is repressing him, he cannot vent his spite in a concentrated way; he is generally spiteful. We would call his brooding consciousness the repressed inwardness of one who should be able to see his situation in terms of the infinite judgment of God or of human love. The Underground Man himself certainly does not see it this way. He does not even know why his age is the age of over-consciousness. Nor does he connect inertia with the social conditions of his life and of Russia in the mid-nineteenth century. Even Dostoevsky at this time did no more than remind readers that this anonymous man could be anyone. The solution that the Underground Man reaches for in his spite is very different from the solution of Mr. Golyadkin.

While Mr. Golyadkin dreams of marrying a rich official's daughter, the Underground Man has dreams too, "dreams of faith, hope, love, the good and the beautiful." He says, "It is worth noting that these attacks of the good and the beautiful visited me even during the period of dissipation and just at the times when I was touching the bottom." This is the first symptom of doubleness, a simultaneity of good and evil. Mr. Golyadkin does not show this symptom. The basic difference is that the Underground Man not only has some idea of his predicament, he tries to meet it by acting spitefully. It is one thing to hurt someone deliberately, it is another to hurt someone deliberately and both enjoy and loathe doing so. The Underground Man's spite is not pretense; he really is spiteful. And in this he may appear like *l'homme de ressentiment* that both Kierkegaard and Nietzsche wrote about. But he is not bourgeois. He does not resent other people being more distinguished than himself; he resents their indifference to him. He resents living in a world where there is no place for him. He does not resent other persons; he resents the fact that he cannot be taken for a person too, and not just as a minor official in an office force. No wonder he does not want to do what is expected of him, to be a good citizen and virtuous. He does not care for somebody else's notions of what is to his advantage. As far as he can understand his own wants, all he needs is to act freely. But we can see that he is already not dependent on anyone. Why then does he worry about independence? Because he confuses independence with his real need, recognition, love. All he owns is his pride, and the refusal to succumb to what is expected of him. The conflict in him between his pride and his need for recognition is accordingly expressed in the form most flattering to pride as a need for independence.

The Underground Man would like to demonstrate his independence and at the same time be recognized, without giving anything of himself, by crushing someone else who would, if he cared, crush him. But the young blood he tested this on pushed him aside without noticing him. What such a lonely pride needs is a love that will both comfort him with recognition and attract his energies away from self-isolation. The prostitute Liza, who comes to him with gratitude and love, only draws on herself the malice of a weak man who has become so wounded by the anonymity of his life and spitefulness that his only possible relationship to someone else is treating her as he has been treated, as a thing. Love comes to him, and he realizes his need for it, too late. Too late he runs after her into the street, "to ask her forgiveness." Too late he suffers from remorse. And yet in his misery he never doubts that even had he found her, he would have treated her spitefully again. Spite is his way of life.

The Underground Man never speaks of God, and he does not say he wants to be loved. If inwardness can be repressed, if decisiveness can be withheld or frustrated, why should not the very consciousness of inwardness be suppressed too? The Underground Man cannot reach out for the right solution to his predicament, and he knows this. But he does not know his predicament completely either. Did Dostoevsky himself at this time? Or was Dostoevky only sure that sadism and masochism are responses to a repressive climate that many were already conditioned by?

The Underground Man, conscious of his own emptiness and isolation, resents himself as well as his society. Having no experience of a society which is a community rather than a bureaucracy, how could he be expected to surrender to anyone when the opportunity comes? He can respond only with the character that his society expects of him, anonymously, without regard for personal feelings. When he says that he cannot think of love except as tyrannizing over someone else (foreshadowing Sartre), we understand that he is not likely to learn from a prostitute. The Underground Man is Dostoevsky's first serious diabolic character, the first to make a self-conscious attempt to define his own fate. But he does not yet know all the terms of reference of this fate. He has not been able to see his situation more clearly because no one else can either. Without a shared experience, or shared inquiry, without a more developed philosophical preparation, man is left with the only measure he does possess, his pride. The next best course then is the one the Underground Man takes, the destructive and self-destructive career of resentment, revenge, sadism-masochism. In the society in which Dostoevsky was living, it was not unusual to say that nihilism is the only way of preserving one's self-respect. "Everyone loves evil," "sin is sweet"—these are phrases from a later novel, but they express a leaning towards the abyss of nihilism which appears for the first time in literature, after the Renaissance is well over and modern times under way. It is a course that romantic isolation as a whole took. In Dostoevsky's novels, however, it was a carefully designed response to the anonymity of life in a disintegrating society. Nihilism had become a game for the overfed and the under-recognized alike.

The double's simultaneity shatters the Aristotelian law of contradiction, for he loves and hates at the same time. Of course, this is not the first time the law had been broken; it had been shattered also in the Pauline conception of original sin. "For that which I do, I allow not. For what I would, that do I not; but what I hate, that I do." Kierkegaard also had maintained that Aristotle's law was binding only on reason, not on the personality as a whole. The Incarnation, two natures in one person, is the sharpest affront of all to reason. Nothing made Kierkegaard more exasperated than his contemporaries' inability to see the impossibility of a rational acceptance of the Incarnation. But the double not only predicates contraries of the same thing at the same time, he breaks the classical ethical principle that no man does evil knowingly. So logic and ethics topple together. The double does evil knowingly and exultingly. He wants to hurt, even destroy, what he loves most. He has no doubt as to what he loves and how much. And one cannot excuse his immorality by suggesting that he loves himself more. Dostoevsky began to write of doubleness of this kind only after he himself had lived with criminals in Siberia. The simultaneity of the double, and the double's attraction to evil, are themes that haunted him the rest of his life. All he adds is the metaphysical structure of inwardness as he later came to see it.

The Underground Man, in the name of over-consciousness, objects to being bound, in an age of reflection, to what is rational, what is expected of him. He does not want to be "some sort of impossible, generalized man." He says that men in his day are oppressed at being men—men with a real individual body and blood. He objects not only to the nineteenth century; he objects to civilization itself. Perhaps reason loses its appeal when it is left in man without a supporting order of reality independent of the mind, an order which can justify both man and reason. Without such an order the sensitive individual does not know even how to express his loneliness except as over-consciousness. In this manner the Underground Man's brooding is the closest he can get to real inwardness. But it is inwardness all the same, because he knows that he is on trial, even though he does not want to, and will not, accept external judgment of himself. He knows life as a series of situations in which recognition and meaning are for unexplained reasons missing; he keeps his head clear by supplying his own justification, acting the stranger at the same time he feels remorseful for being so. But his characteristic resentment indicates that he has an instinct for a different kind of life in which spite would be neither possible nor necessary. He does not bring such a life to the front of his mind where he could have it to choose or reject. He rejects, e.g., in Liza, an opportunity, not a way of life. As the bourgeois is caught in a mesh of his own conventions, so the Underground Man, rising deliberately above the insane fate of the bourgeois Golyadkin, is repelled by the routines and anonymity of modern life which allow the good and the lovely to come to man only accidentally.

THE SPIDER IN THE BATHHOUSE

One of the curious things about Dostoevsky's portrayals of doubleness is that he seems never to have been fully satisfied with his own explanations. Each novel adds something. The Underground Man does evil as a protest against the evil of his own isolation. He does not like evil, and he does not do it to gain some advantage for himself. He may be a sadist, but he is not a matter-of-fact sensualist, like Prince Valkovsky of *The Insulted and Injured*. This repulsive creature boasts of his adherence to the principle that "At the root of all human virtues lies the completest egoism." "I'm fond of secret hidden vice," he confesses to an innocent youth [prototype of Arkady in *The Raw Youth*], "even a little filthy for variety." What does it matter whether Dostoevsky may have liked a little filthy vice himself? Unlike Prince Valkovsky, whose conscience seems to have been completely quiet, Dostoevsky had the tormented conscience of a double who hates what he loves, and loves what he hates. A typical sensualist, like a typical political nihilist (Peter Verhovensky. in *The Possessed*), is satisfied with himself; Dostoevsky himself was not.

The most curious case in all his novels is that of the mask-like figure Svidrigailov in *Crime and Punishment*. He is neither double nor sensualist. He is enough of a sensualist to disgust young Raskolnikov, but he may not disgust the readers of the book who can see the pathos of the man. He is an enigma, not only because he tries to hide his lust for Raskolnikov's sister but because he does not let anyone know until near the end that he really does want to be loved by Dounia. Perhaps one might say that the simultaneity of lust and the yearning to be loved is another, and normal, ambivalence of the double. But there would seem to be little reason to look for repressed inwardness in Svidrigailov. He is a calculating creature where immediate ends are concerned but knows next to nothing of his predicament as a human being. When Dounia finally refuses to marry him, even when she realizes that he wants her love, he can think of nothing else but to arrange his fortune for the benefit of others and then kill himself. His portrayal is a masterly account of a person who is just as much an enigma to himself as to others, but who is even in his sensuality more to be pitied than disliked.

If Svidrigailov's pursuits are not metaphysically significant, his imagination at any rate is memorable. He tells Raskolnikov that "As soon as one is ill, as soon as the normal earthly order of the organism is broken, one begins to realize the possibility of another world; and the more seriously ill one is, the closer becomes one's contact with that other world." Is this the sickness unto death which Kierkegaard said was that despair into which a man falls when he is conscious of his inescapable sinfulness? Svidrigailov knows only the sickness of the psychological organism when the will is weakened and the subconscious mind is free to speak. He certainly has no sense of God or sin, and there is no evidence that he ever longed for eternity. But he could fancy eternity. "We always imagine eternity as something beyond our conception, something vast. Why must it be vast? Instead of all that, what if it's one little room, like a bathhouse in the country, black and grimy and spiders in every corner, and that's all eternity is?" Even when he thinks of eternity, Svidrigailov cannot rise above the image of a spider in a bathhouse. Nor can he conceive of eternity save in terms of some opposite, the repulsive, shabby buildings with insect residents on a provincial estate. Svidrigailov is enigmatic just because he combines such opposites in himself without being aware of what their presence in him means. Kierkegaard, no doubt, would have called him an aesthete.

Without knowing what he is doing, Svidrigailov undercuts the usual view of eternity. Dostoevsky's doubles always undercut values, believing and disbelieving, loving and hating at the same time. The frankest expression of this is always made by the most talkative persons in his tales. But they are not the ones who always understand most. In their explicitness they stand somewhere in between the Underground Man and Ivan Karamazov. Arkady Dolgoruky, for instance, says:

> I had the soul of a spider. . . . Let the reader remember the soul of the spider, in the man who longed to get away from them all and from the whole world for the sake of seemliness. The longing for seemliness was still there, of course, and very intense, but how could it be linked with other longings of a very different sort is a mystery to me. It always has been a mystery and I have marvelled a thousand times at that faculty in man of cherishing in his soul his loftiest ideal side by side with the most abject baseness and all quite sincerely.

The image of the spider reappears, joined with love of seemliness, and both are linked mysteriously in man, and especially in Russians. Dostoevsky guessed that this doubleness is a universal disposition, but he supposed also that Russians in his century were especially sensitive to it. Could he have been trying to justify some sickness of his own? Is this what Baudelaire also was attempting, as Sartre has suggested, by holding that "the invocation to God or spirituality is a desire to mount in the scale, that of Satan or animality is a joy in going downwards." Whatever the status of Dostoevsky's motives, we should not fail to remark the juxtaposition of seemliness with the

grimy spider. Dostoevsky was an odd mixture of prudery and grov-
elling abandonment of self-respect. How much he must have been
hurt, must have wanted to hurt himself each time he behaved unseemly! For this strange man had the tender-minded scrupulosity
of a petty bourgeois, the same scrupulosity which we meet in the
thief Dmitri Karamazov who says the one thing he could not do is to
steal.

Dmitri, like Arkady, sees life in simple extremes coexisting.
"When I do leap into the pit, I go headlong with my heels up, and
am pleased to be falling in that degrading attitude, and pride myself
upon it. And in the very depths of that degradation I begin a hymn
of praise." He is the one who says, "Here the boundaries meet and
all the contradictions exist side by side." In man, he observes, the
ideal of the Madonna exists side by side with the ideal of Sodom.
And of Dmitri, the prosecutor at his trial said, "He seems to represent
Russia as she is . . . he is spontaneous, he is a marvellous mingling
of good and evil." But we may still speculate that this is an excuse
Dostoevsky is making for himself too. Dmitri may have been spontaneous, but was his author? Certainly the Underground Man was
not; and we may wonder how caprice, as a response to repression,
can be succeeded by spontaneity. Besides, does even Dostoevsky
want us to believe that Dmitri is spontaneous? He is passionate,
gay, and easily depressed, above all irresponsible. Is not this irresponsibility perhaps an unconscious expression not of a free nature
but of a nature under stress of a life it cannot understand?

And even if Dmitri's spontaneity is not a planned way out, but
only an instinctive attempt to mimic freedom, Dmitri's doubleness,
like that of the Underground Man, is an excuse for not being able to
accept the judgment of eternity. We know that when Dmitri, himself
in custody, dreamed himself in circumstances justifying a pity he
himself had never shown, he was still not able to learn the lesson of
pity once he had awakened. The truth about Dmitri is not the verbal
simultaneity which he knows by rote, but his inability to understand
why he, and perhaps other Russians, had this darkness in them at

this particular time. In accepting this as a universal disposition he avoids the self-questioning and judgment that he needs most.

PRIDE, PITY, AND RESURRECTION

An imaginative sensualist like Dmitri can sometimes express an ambivalence that he has not fully experienced. Has that one really spent much time thinking about the ideal of the Madonna? And how often has he sung his hymn of praise to God? He is a rhetorical sentimentalist, but not an honest man. He is not intelligent enough to see that he is quibbling even when he professes to be an honest man. Dostoevsky holds out no hope for sensualists, not only for Prince Valkovsky and Fyodor Karamazov, but Svidrigailov and Dmitri. Why? Could it be because sensualists are not intelligent enough to understand their predicaments? They are imaginative enough, however, to avoid coming to terms with inwardness. Dmitri's fondness for the contradictions that exist side by side is his way of excusing his own shallowness and irresponsibility. It is not the way that Raskolnikov or Stavroguin or Ivan choose to explain their dilemmas.

Crime and Punishment is not only the first of Dostoevsky's stories in which religion plays any part, it is the first in which the double's dilemma is worked out in terms of inwardness. It is also the only novel in which a double is purged. Is Raskolnikov really a double, and does he exhibit affective and moral ambivalence? Or is he rather more like Julien Sorel who has to struggle with two parts of his personality, his head and his heart? Raskolnikov does indeed wobble back and forth between the claims of pride and pity. Like Julien Sorel he understands that the interior battle is essentially between reason as an instrument of the ego's desire for power and glory, and the heart's sorrow for others.

In Julien Sorel the conflict darts from head to heart and back again. He willfully represses his heart in order to achieve worldly attention. Does not Raskolnikov do the same? He represses pity as long as it gets in the way of the egoism that his rational crime is fed by. But he never denies the necessity of pity. "Pain and suffering are always inevitable for a large intelligence and a deep heart. The really great men must, I think, have great sadness on earth." Not only does he never deny pity, he is constantly tortured by his Titanic pride. He has an instinct within him that solemnly condemns him even while he refuses to listen. In Raskolnikov too the contradictions exist side by side. Repression only acts to elevate one side, it does not make the other any less active. Time after time Raskolnikov's pity produces works of compassion, charity, and self-sacrifice. What makes his simultaneity or doubleness look different is that his reason remains active on one level, and pity on another.

Yet pity is not so repressed it has to explode and destroy the man, as Julien Sorel's heart finally rebelled against his reason. Raskolnikov is obsessed by the enormity of what he is about to do; Julien is disturbed only after his failure to kill the woman he loved. And only in prison does Julien conceive, even for a moment, of eternity as a possible measure of life. From the first page of *Crime and Punishment* the hero is "sick," "frightened," "irritable," "overstrained"; but Julien becomes aware of his own hypocrisy, his form of repression, only in prison. *Crime and Punishment* is the story of the half-conscious debate of inwardness rising slowly and surely to a fully conscious plane. Raskolnikov confesses to the police, not because he has failed or been caught, but because he knows he cannot resolve the torment of his questionableness or suppress the inward debate.

He knows that the debate between reason and pity has a religious context. When he hears once more the story of the raising of Lazarus, he realizes that he himself is dead as long as pity is suppressed by reason. Sonia too knows that he must be resurrected, and that without her help he will not be able to pass through his isolation. Her compassion is a human participation in the divine charity. And she believes in this charity. "What should I be without God?" It was her father Marmeladov who asked Raskolnikov, "Do you know what it is to have nowhere to turn?" Sonia is the one to whom he turns, not because he loves her but because she first loves him. "The murderer and the harlot," one who has killed someone else's life, the other who has killed chastity, join forces, but not, as Raskolnikov thinks, because they are "both accursed," but because she has faith in the love of Christ to raise both of them from the grave. She had become a prostitute to save her family, and he a murderer to demonstrate a power worthy of his pride.

Raskolnikov uses the conflict between reason and pity as a release from the same threat of anonymity that troubles the Underground Man. He would resist this pressure not merely to exist but to have power. He wants not recognition but the assurance that he is fully autonomous. He comes to realize that autonomy is not a livable antithesis to anonymity, but is as lethal as anonymity. The only practical answer to the thrust of anonymity is the mutual recognition that takes place in a religiously motivated compassion. Why does Raskolnikov experience this compassion while the Underground Man does not? It would be comforting to say that it was because Dostoevsky dictated *Crime and Punishment* to a fine young woman whom he married shortly after. But in terms of the two stories themselves it looks as if the Underground Man did not have the full religious context in which to place his egoism, his rebellion against anonymity, and his unconfessed need for recognition. Even where the context and the need are understood, as in the later novels, the will is not purified as it is in *Crime and Punishment*. What this novel has which the later novels do not have is the compassion of Sonia, the believer in Resurrection. Could we expect her to be re-created? She is not in herself implausible, but her circumstances are. Is salvation to be met only through harlots? Or does Dostoevsky mean to show how improbable salvation by compassion is at all, since it depends on chance?

The two doubles in *The Possessed*, Stavroguin and Kirillov, are not saved at all. Both commit suicide, Stavroguin, like Svidrigailov, because he despairs of living without love, and Kirillov, like Raskolnikov, because he would kill in order to prove his right to live. But Stavroguin, unlike Svidrigailov, was not looking for love—Liza offered herself anyway—but was hoping that her sacrifice of honor might awaken a dormant power of love in him. Kirillov, unlike Raskolnikov, killed himself instead of someone else, ostensibly to prove his superhuman courage to do the one thing no man wants to do, but actually to save himself from the torment of living in a world without a Resurrection. Kirillov, like Raskolnikov and Ivan, holds reason more authoritative than God or pity, and like them he would build his life on a great chance. The Grand Inquisitor is just as thoroughgoing a nihilist as Kirillov or Raskolnikov, and he too would kill, if necessary, for the sake of humanity.

But both Ivan and Raskolnikov are more normal than Kirillov who is not only epileptic—like Prince Myshkin in *The Idiot*—but so obsessed by his perverse logic that he appears pathological at times. Kirillov lights a candle before the holy ikon in his room, and occasionally plays with the landlady's child. He has given up his profession of engineering and spends his time at home constructing a watertight reason for suicide. Stavroguin, nobleman, ex-Guards officer (reminding us of Tolstoy's Dolakhov and Lermontov's Pechorin) reflects more clearly than any other character in Dostoevsky's novels the gentry's boredom and loss of faith in their class. Like them he has tried everything and finds nothing to replace noblesse oblige. Having no sense of obligation, he substitutes its opposites, debauchery and caprice. He hurts others without cause, hoping to find in evil some responsibility. He is incapable of love and yet knows that love is his only chance. All that seems open to him is evil. He has seduced a child, and her shame haunts him until he can bear remembering her no longer and kills himself. He has needed nobility of heart, but he denies obligation and perishes.

Stavroguin is a proper name built on the Greek word "stavros" or cross. Bishop Tihon tells him that "the fundamental idea of your document is a terrible, undisguised need of punishment, the need of the cross, of public chastisement. Meanwhile, this need of the cross in a man who doesn't believe in the cross—why, that in itself is an idea." Stavroguin himself says that he "seeks measureless suffering," but he cannot accept the kind of suffering that is secret and silent. He wants to suffer for all to see, and he has no faith that he will be forgiven. As he has hurt others immeasurably, so he would hurt himself. He cannot rise from the self-isolation in which he has entombed his personality. He cannot even hear God discussed by Bishop Tihon without irritation and embarrassment. Unlike Kirillov he does not love Christ, nor would he believe even if he could. He thinks wholly in human terms, as Kirillov thinks almost in divine terms. One complements the other. And indeed Kirillov's function in part is to put Stavroguin's dilemma into words.

To the least human of the conspirators, Peter Verhovensky, Stavroguin may be a prince in disguise, "Ivan the Tsarevitch," who will lead Russia after it is "overwhelmed with darkness," and the earth is weeping "for its old gods." To the rest he is the epitome of compulsive nihilism. He insists that he is always responsible for what he does, and he may have been responsible for almost all he did, although sometimes he appears to act in a daze. He is observant, unlike Kirillov, and reticent; he does not try to explain himself to everyone he meets; he is too conscious of the improbability that he can be forgiven. Both he and Kirillov are unhappy from their awareness of the vacuum left in them by the departure of the old gods, too unhappy to go on living. Kirillov, less profound than his puppet master, goes on repeating Stavroguin's iconoclastic logic long after Stavroguin has lost interest. There is no Sonia for either of them. And if there were, Stavroguin's refusal to take up the cross would have kept her compassion at arm's length. Kirillov, victim of another man's metaphysical game, finally slips beyond human touch. There is a deep pathos in his childlike despair over the dead Christ he loved.

In *The Raw Youth* Dostoevsky attempted once again to describe the course from doubleness to integrity. But this time he did not pretend that he had succeeded. Versilov, one of the most enigmatic of Dostoevsky's characters, and the only one to speak of himself as split into two selves, is a mystery to everyone he meets. Like Stavroguin he is in the center of every circle; people wait for him to reveal his special secret. And like Stavroguin he does not think in religious terms, but sets his hope on the love of a proud young woman who cannot respond to him when he really needs her. And like Stavroguin again he is loved by a meek woman, to whom he returns in the end to linger out his life. Versilov is not only a split personality, in a clinical sense; he has the Underground Man's affective ambivalence. In a moment of frenzy he tries to kill Katerina whom he adores. The narrator, however, rejects insanity as the cause, he says he accepts the theory of a "second self." This self is "the first stage of serious mental derangement." Versilov is deranged indeed, and yet the narrator states that "even though the 'second self' did come in, it was partly a whim . . . . But all this is only my theory, it would be hard to decide for certain."

Versilov himself has less difficulty in accepting this theory. "Do you know, I feel as though I were split in two? Yes, I am really split in two mentally, and I'm horribly afraid of it. It's just as though one's second self were standing beside one. One is sensible and rational oneself, but the other self is impelled to do something perfectly senseless, and sometimes very funny." And sometimes horrible too. In Versilov we see Mr. Golyadkin once again for a moment. And yet Versilov, like Stavroguin, can dream innocently of an earthly paradise where all is clear and quiet. And like Stavroguin he acts compulsively. After his frenzied attempt to shoot Katerina whom he both loved and hated, he tried to kill himself. When he recovered, his second self had fortunately disappeared—his son says that "all his intellect and moral nature have remained unchanged." He is now "good natured and candid as a child." He is no longer Versilov either. This can hardly be called a new life; it is another man living his life for him, supported by a rich aunt. Dostoevsky had only succeeded in painting one more portrait of a nobleman in whom the consciousness of inwardness cannot be made explicit.

It is clear from the remarks at the end of *The Raw Youth* that Dostoevsky had hoped to show something of the new life that he had foreshadowed at the end of *Crime and Punishment*, and which he returns to in *The Brothers Karamazov*. "If I had been a Russian novelist, I should certainly have chosen my heroes from the old nobility, because only in that type of cultivated Russian is it possible to find at least that outward semblance of fine order and aesthetic beauty so necessary in a novel. I am not joking when I say this, although I am not a nobleman myself." What he felt the need of were "completely worked-out forms of honor and duty that never existed anywhere in Russia except in the nobility, even in the most rudimentary shape. I speak as a calm man seeking calm." He spoke as a disquieted man seeking calm, and not as a nobleman. "What to my mind is of most consequence is the finality of the forms and the existence of some sort of order not prescribed from above, but developed from within. . . . What matters most of all for us is to have any sort of order of our own . . . instead of this everlasting destruction, instead of chips flying in all directions, rubbish and disorder that have led to nothing for two hundred years." He excuses his inability to write an artistically satisfying novel in *The Raw Youth* by saying that the types of people he has had to write of are "transitory, and so a novel about them cannot have artistic finish . . . one would have to guess too much." These are the types generated in a time of "lawlessness and chaos," and whatever one says about them, no matter how autobiographical, will be hypothetical. It is one thing to accept schizophrenic symptoms as pathological and leave it to doctors to find the causes; it is another to use the symptoms as hasty, half-baked efforts to find a satisfying response to a world of lawlessness and chaos. Just as the writer Dostoevsky moves from one situation to another, carrying different bags to different trains, so his characters respond differently to the situations they are put in. Chaos and anonymity breed doubleness and self-paralysis. He was too honest an artist to depict much resurrection.

IVAN'S CONDITIONALISM

Dmitri Karamazov can imagine more than the Underground Man, but he is even less responsible. Dmitri's imagination is passionate and yet rather static, pictorial in a cliché manner. The ideal of the Madonna is posed side by side with the ideal of Sodom. He does not elaborate. But Ivan who has a richer imagination, makes up the parables (he calls them "poems") of The Geological Cataclysm and The Grand Inquisitor to achieve a moral disengagement from images and arguments in which he cannot wholly believe. Like his brother Dmitri he knows too much about the poles of his dilemma to think of affective ambivalence as a possible way out. He thinks of almost everything else first: "Everything is lawful," the Grand Inquisitor's totalitarianism, a church-state, metaphysical rebellion, Titanism. But what is most characteristic about his mind is its conditionalism. He puts everything as an hypothesis, a superior sort of guess. If this, then such and such follows. But Ivan can accept neither premise nor any of the conclusions. Like all the doubles he is suspended between two irreconcilables; in his case, his love of freedom and his longing for justice.

As he has diagnosed the state of the world, injustice exists because man is free. In order to get justice, man may have to give up freedom. If he could believe in a justly ordained society, such as a theocracy, there would be no problem. If man were willing to give up his freedom, there would be no problem either; everything could be arranged by church or state. If he could live on indignation and rebellion, he might accept the world as it is, as both paradoxical and terrible. If he insists on remaining free, he must take the consequences. If he could forget justice, he could regard "everything as lawful." If he could think only of his own freedom, might not justice come of itself? Ivan cannot believe in a solution that does not satisfy both realities: the freedom which he knows in himself as a young man who has risen in the world in spite of an indifferent father, and his longing for justice which as philosopher and orphan he cannot be ignorant of. He respects reason, and knows the need for pity. But as with Raskolnikov—even more so—his reason is stronger than his pity. Unlike Raskolnikov, Ivan never pities individuals. He would like to love them, but like the Grand Inquisitor he can only love humanity whom he would deprive of freedom. He sees the need for justice but can understand it only in terms of social planning, never as personal compassion. He is intelligent enough, however, to foresee that totalitarian justice cannot replace the humble acceptance of the suffering of others, that indeed it may even take away the freedom of those it pretends to help.

With Ivan we return to the world of Kierkegaard's paradoxes. In Kierkegaard's view the great paradox was the Incarnation. For Ivan it is a confrontation of a supposedly just God with his impossibly just world. And this was as morally offensive to Dostoevsky as the Incarnation is intellectually contradictory. Kierkegaard thought that man's ultimate choice must be the choice of accepting this paradox in all its paradoxicality or remaining shut up within himself.

He himself both chose and held back. But the choice was not thereby made invalid. Nor was the object of the choice intellectualized; it was present and very real. For Dostoevsky and his characters the situation of man in the nineteenth century is quite different. Even in Ivan who knows almost everything the choice is not between two real beings, the self or God; it is between two subjective principles, freedom and the longing for justice.

The difference is important. In the Dostoevsky heroes the reality of man's dilemma is transformed into subjective dispositions. Another way of saying this is to say that their inwardness has been repressed. Kierkegaardian inwardness is an awareness of the reality of infinite as well as finite, of the reality of a judge in a real trial. Dostoevskian inwardness is a brooding over instincts which cannot break through to the plane of acceptance or belief. There would be no brooding, of course, if there were no acceptance of the misery of human life lived in "lawlessness and chaos," in a civilization which dehumanizes. Man's refusal to accept life on these terms—and most men cannot—is a sign of an awareness that has only its own subjective yearnings to justify itself. The man who feels this way about himself will use the poles of his dilemma to justify a situation which he cannot radically alter. Doubleness by itself is not a way out of the period of isolation; it is only self-justification. Caught in its own circle, it wears itself out or gives up.

THE DEMONIACAL

Dostoevsky's admission that "the second self" is a whim, is a way of saying that doubleness is a controlled response to repressed inwardness. And it is probably a fairer way of explaining experience that is not understood by a fictional character as clearly as it is by the student who reads about him. It is when we compare Dostoevsky's doubleness with similar manifestations that Kierkegaard analysed, that we see how necessary it is to distinguish in terms of the deliberate and the compulsive. In *The Concept of Dread* he discussed the correlative experiences of dread of the good and dread of the evil, the experiences of the demoniacal and original sin. St. Paul's formula for the latter could be a formula for affective and moral ambivalence. But St. Paul explains this as "sin dwelling in me." It is not deliberate, not a response to a situation or a time. It is "the bondage of sin," or as Kierkegaard put it, "an unfree relation to evil." Man is pulled toward evil, whether he wishes or no. But Dostoevsky's doubles thrust themselves gloatingly into the heart of evil. Neither Kierkegaard nor orthodox Christian theology has anything to say about this conscious caprice. Original sin, pathological diabolism, and the double's caprice are not the same at all.

The dread of the good or the demoniacal, "the unfree relation to the good," is the rejection of that which is most loved, just as the dread of the evil is the reaching out for the evil which one hates most. The demoniacal is a compulsive principle which Kierkegaard describes in certain situations, nor does he say that it is seized as a response, even a whim, to a dilemma. He only says, "The demoniacal does not shut itself up with something, but shuts itself up . . . unfreedom makes a prisoner of itself." And he goes on to say that "the only power that can compel shut-upness to speak, is either a higher demon or the good which is absolutely able to be silent." When we recall that Kierkegaard had spoken of his self-isolation as demoniacal, and that he had never been able to explain why he could not break it, we can see why he did not realize that the demoniacal is not possession but obsession.

In *The Possessed* Dostoevsky used the New Testament analogy of the possessed men and the swine who received their demons. But he understood that men are possessed by an environment which they have fashioned, and that the form of their possession will express their search of the very life that their environment discourages them from leading. If Kierkegaard had understood that the demoniacal may be a free relation to evil as well as an unfree relation, he could be said to have understood doubleness also. As it was, he seems to have known the demoniacal as compulsive, not connecting it even in *The Concept of Dread* with self-isolation. But he pointed out at least the connection between the demoniacal and inwardness. "If inwardness is lacking, the spirit is finitized. Inwardness is, therefore, eternity, or the determinant of the eternal in a man." "But men are not willing to think eternity seriously, they dread it, and dread discovers a hundred ways of escape. But this precisely is the demoniacal." In other words, there is a Dostoevskian demonism, capricious, fully conscious, and a Kierkegaardian demonism that does not know what it is doing. Both are ways of escaping responsibility and God.

Kierkegaardian dread and the demoniacal are bourgeois ways of escape, not ways out for men who have completely rejected bourgeois ways of life. Where self-isolation is concerned Kierkegaard was personally vulnerable. Unlike Dostoevsky he was able to make a clear decision to accept a transcendent God whose ways are past finding out. And yet he could not break out of his self-isolation to accept that God's forgiveness. He understood the demoniacal as self-enclosure; he judged self-isolation as compulsive; and yet he seems to have thought of the demoniacal in origin as a bourgeois evasion of the very inwardness he himself experienced. The dread of evil, original sin, is according to Kierkegaard a universal anxiety. But dread of the good is not universal. It arises as a response to certain situations, one of which Kierkegaard has defined, and which Dostoevsky analysed repeatedly. Whether compulsive and demoniacal, or deliberate and capricious, whether bourgeois' or double's, dread of the good has become since Kierkegaard's time an experience which millions are caught up in. New anxieties have appeared, new situations confront man. "He therefore who has learned rightly to be in dread has learned the most important thing." It would seem that in this respect Dostoevsky had learned more than Kierkegaard.

CHAPTER 5

The Destruction of God

"You have only to get rid of the idea of God in man."—Dostoevsky

"Wretched man, your God lies in the dust broken to fragments, and serpents dwell around him. And now you love even the serpents for his sake."—Nietzsche

THE DOUBLE DID NOT invent moral and religious chaos, he found it all around him. Hegel said, "Nature bears traces of a lost God everywhere, both in man and outside him." Neither Nietzsche nor Dostoevsky referred to God as lost, but as murdered, and murdered in the nineteenth century. Each in his way accepted God's death as a cultural fact; each in his own way gave more thought to the resurrection of man than to the resurrection of God. They took this second death of God as seriously as the disciples at the Crucifixion, but only because they were afraid that man would also die without a God to keep him alive. Nietzsche himself rejoiced because he was convinced that with God out of the way man could replace him in importance. Dostoevsky, while accepting with equanimity the death of a transcendent power he could not understand, saw more clearly some of the frightening alternatives open to mankind.

Perhaps Dostoevsky's relative detachment was that of an artist; it was also part and parcel of a mind that had experienced the death of God in himself. He grew up in a society turbulent with political, social, and ideological change; destructive ideas were in the air, conspirators gathering, discussing, aspiring. He himself was arrested, condemned to death, reprieved, sent to Siberia for a term. Brought up in an age in which nothing was too sacred to be preserved without rational justification, Dostoevsky could not simply take God's absence for granted. No individual could be responsible for the death of God, and yet so close to an age of faith were Dostoevsky and his contemporaries that it seemed plausible to them that each of them had had some part in the removal by reason of the idea of ideas that had unified mind and existence for so long. Therefore, "I killed God." First kill God, and then take a second look at man.

Dostoevsky's first literary response to this world, as recorded in *Poor Folk*, recommended humility and self-sacrifice. But he must have been persuaded by his crucial personal experiences in prison that neither humility nor self-sacrifice can speak to the decadent society which had provoked conspiracy and rebellion. Until he found a more plausible ground for the exercise of self-sacrifice and humility, he turned to the initial reaction to decadence, rebellion and its advocates. These do not all know that God is dead, or even that he must be removed. Some, like the Underground Man, know only that their revolutionary society makes personal security uncertain. Few yet realize the depth of that uncertainty. Dostoevsky himself did not plunge into the metaphysical depths until he wrote *Crime and Punishment*, and oddly enough did not connect the death of God with the Russian chaos until he wrote *The Possessed*. Only in the last novel, *The Brothers Karamazov*, did he explicitly relate revolution and God.

Atheism on a large scale did not appear for the first time either in Russia or in the nineteenth century. Indeed announcements about the death of God were not typical atheistic statements. Those who said "God is dead" were not saying "There is no God" in mocking terms; they were not talking of God at all, but rather of a cultural fact. When asked by his father, Ivan Karamazov replies that there is no God. But he is not at all troubled by the question of existence or non-existence as a philosophical question. What does trouble him is the consequence of an idea, in his case the idea of a just, all-powerful being existing side by side with his own barbaric, chaotic world. This is why Dostoevsky makes no effort to prove or disprove in any of his novels the existence of God. God is an abstraction, almost only a word; but his influence or non-influence is real and experiential.

We do not know the history of Nietzsche's religious development from childhood, from a Lutheran parson's family to his education in classical humanism in German universities. It may never have occurred to Nietzsche that there might be a God, after a Santa Claus-like emancipation from childhood myths. Certainly as a mature man he affected an indifference to the question of God's existence worthy of his mentor Stendhal. What struck him as interesting was that so many other people still thought they needed a God. And it seemed to him, in part because of his admiration for Greek humanism, that life would be uncluttered and joyful if man could learn to rid himself of any dependence on a non-existent being. Just as the Grand Inquisitor was annoyed with Christ for returning to earth to interfere with the new humanism, so Nietzsche was indignant that a phantom, long since intellectually discredited, should linger in the minds of his contemporaries. The time had long passed when men could be proud of having been made in the image of God; and the time had come when the only question was whether man was to be a usurper or a successor.

How Nietzsche liked to call himself "the anti-Christ!" And by now, the middle of the twentieth century, the very sentence "God is dead" is associated with his name. He uttered it in writing for the first time in 1881 in *The Joyful Wisdom*. Even so, Dostoevsky had anticipated him in this as in so much else, Dostoevsky "the only person who has taught me anything about psychology . . . and I have vowed a queer kind of gratitude to him, although he goes against my deepest instincts." It was ten years earlier, in *The Possessed* that Dostoevsky introduced the same theme. Nietzsche may have read this book, although it may not have been translated in time. It appears likely that Nietzsche had read *The House of the Dead, The Gambler, The Insulted and Injured, Notes from Underground*. He may have read also—or have heard something about— *Crime and Punishment* and *The Idiot*. There is no evidence at all that he was inspired by Dostoevsky to say "God is dead." It is more likely that he was echoing Hegel and Heine, or parodying the New Testament itself.

Dostoevsky, through Kirillov, alludes to the first Good Friday, the day God died on the cross for mankind. Nietzsche simply ignores the death on Calvary and never associates God with Christ. The Incarnation meant much less to him than to Kirillov, even as an idea. And yet Nietzsche probably had heard Luther's chorale, "God himself is dead," and been taught the Christian explanation so simply spoken by Angelus Silesius: "God dies in order to live in thee." He had no difficulty thinking of the mythical Dionysos as a dead and resurrected God, but choked on Christ. Whatever his reason for parodying religion, his conclusion was that God is dead so that man can live without him. Père de Lubac was right in saying that when Nietzsche said, "God is dead," "it is not a mere statement of fact. It expresses a choice." This was the man who also said, "What would there be left to create if there were any Gods?" Having never been seriously tempted to believe, he could afford to be flippant. Of Dostoevsky it must be said that he was one of those men of whom theologians sometimes speak when they say that wanting to believe is itself a sign of belief. If we never learn for sure whether Dostoevsky believed in God, there is no doubt at all that he wanted to.

Both Dostoevsky and Nietzsche link the destruction of God with the destruction of morality. If one disappears, so does the other. For all practical purposes there is no difference between the Law and the Giver of the Law. As Ivan Karamazov puts it in his oracular manner: "For every individual who does not believe in God or immortality the moral law of nature must immediately be changed into the exact contrary of the former religious law." Similarly Nietzsche pronounced that with the collapse of belief in God "our entire European morality" crumbles. Are all atheists or immoralists equally obsessed by the death of God? Apparently not. The fact remains that only Dostoevsky and Nietzsche at the end of their century meditated at any length on this theme. And neither one was aware of its importance when he began his writing career.

The Underground Man does not know God is dead; nor did the author of *Human All Too Human*. Not all doubles knew it, not all free spirits. Raskolnikov and Stavroguin would have understood had they been told, but they do not speak of it. Only Kirillov and Ivan

Karamazov think in large enough terms; only these two are detached enough philosophically to penetrate the secret event of their age. Raskolnikov is only interested in testing himself, Stavroguin in finding himself and a channel for his indubitable power. Neither has time to give to analyzing the conditions which have contributed to his personal crisis. But Kirillov and Ivan are natural intellectuals; ideas are more real to them than persons, story than fact. Beyond these the only other figure in any of the novels who can talk their language—but who is perhaps remembered rather for his deed—is Peter Verhovensky, the chief conspirator who murders Shatov.

Kirillov and Ivan should not be compared too closely. Of the two Ivan is the saner and more rounded. He is incapable either of killing himself or of killing his father, or for that matter putting into practice any of his own schemes. Kirillov affects indifference to the fate of others and speaks of his own suicide as if he were talking about someone else, but we know he is terribly afraid to die. It is very difficult to wipe from one's mind the suspicion that he must have been insane to practice what he had preached, so unusual is the committing of a rational crime against oneself. Without Ivan's education, speaking almost as ventriloquist dummy for Stavroguin, his weird syllogisms could fool no one with an ounce of earthborn ballast. Like Ivan's half brother Smerdyakov, Kirillov's arguments show what happens when reason is divorced from feeling and the prudence that normally guards feeling. But poor Kirillov, as well as Smerdyakov and Peter Verhovensky, really believes that "everything is lawful." Ivan does not, but does not know why either. When God is dead, everything ought to be lawful.

KIRILLOV'S GREAT DAY:
STAVROGUIN'S LAST CHANCE

Kirillov is the first of Dostoevsky's great figures to take the destruction of God as his central idea. "I am bound to show my unbelief . . . I have no higher idea than disbelief in God. I have all the history of mankind on my side. Man has done nothing but to invent God so as to go on living, and not kill himself; that's the whole of universal history up till now. I am the first one in the whole history of mankind who would not invent God. Let them know it once for all." This man is an engineer who does not build, a defected conspirator who cannot be bothered with destroying his country when there is a God to be destroyed. He is not educated well enough to know that if a man is obsessed by some idea, he does not need either history or argument to make him believe in it. And so he himself cannot believe in man until he has demonstrated his disbelief in God. Crazy though he is, at times he sounds like Nietzsche's double, persuaded that man had invented gods and moralities in order to escape his "terrible freedom."

Peter Verhovensky, who never quite understood other people, once remarked that Kirillov believed more thoroughly than a priest. It is true that Kirillov thought that men invented God "so as to go on living." But if there is no God, how can man go on living? "If God exists, all is His will and from His will I cannot escape. If not, it's all my will and I am bound to show my self-will. . . . If there is no God, then I am God." Even if God exists, all may not be His will. And if he does not, there is no will but man's, and man does not have to show self-will. Kirillov was too much of a recluse to know that self-will is not the only will possible for men without God. And if there is no God, then there is no reason to call Kirillov God. Why should he want to? He reasons much like Smerdyakov, who says to Ivan, "In what manner and with what sort of justice can I be held responsible as a Christian in the other world for having denied Christ, when through the very thought alone, before denying Him I had been relieved from my christening?" Could not one of the consequences of disbelief be just this, that men who identify civilization and order with a Divine Ordainer come to think that the withdrawal of God leaves only self-will?

Kirillov is not a run of the mill atheist who does not care whether God exists or not:

Listen to a great idea: there was a day on earth, and in the midst of the earth there stood three crosses. One on the Cross had such faith that he said to another, "Today thou shalt be with me in Paradise." The day ended; both died and passed away and found neither Paradise nor resurrection. His words did not come true. Listen: that Man was the loftiest of all on earth. He was that which gave meaning to life. The whole planet, with everything on it, is mere madness without that Man. There has never been any like Him before or since, never up to a miracle. For that is the miracle, that there never was or will be another like Him. And if that is so, if the laws of nature did not spare even Him, and have not spared even their miracle and made even Him live on a lie and die on a lie, then all the planet is a lie and rests on a lie and on mockery.

The "great idea," the anticipation of Nietzsche's "joyful wisdom," is that there was no resurrection. But there should have been, for "that Man," Christ, "gave meaning to life." And the life that history has embodied ever since His death, has been built on the pretense that there was a resurrection. If the lie is caught, then man has two alternatives. If he does not recognize that he is God's substitute, he ought to be so unhappy that he will kill himself. If he does recognize that he has replaced God, then he "will live in the greatest glory." "But one, the first, must kill himself, for else who will begin and prove it? So I must certainly kill myself to begin and prove it."
- Why does someone have to kill himself to prove that man can be happy without God? Why must self-destruction be the sign of the man-god? From a religious point of view man cannot be understood apart from the God-relationship, the creature from the Creator. And Kirillov's mind is, in spite of its warp, religious. On the one hand, he adores the image of Christ, "the loftiest of all on earth." He thinks that even "God is indispensable, and therefore must exist." On the other hand, although "God has tormented me all my life," he says, "I know that there is no God and there can't be. . . . There is nothing higher for me than the thought that there is no God." Racked by antithetical convictions he concludes, "A man cannot go on living if he believes both things." And so he tries to resolve his dilemma by favoring reason. "It's my duty to make myself believe that I do not believe in God."

Is Kirillov's point of view really religious? Like his author he loves the image of Christ, and there is no doubt that he is miserable without God. "I'm awfully unhappy, for I'm awfully afraid." But his syllogisms clack rather mechanically, and in his heart there is little left but the reverberation of lost belief. This is not enough to live with. And yet why he should feel that he has to prove that he is sovereign by killing himself, especially when he is not yet reconciled to the new sovereignty, is another matter. He shows no other interest in his "terrible freedom"—a phrase he may have borrowed like much else from Stavroguin. He is bogged down in the question whether anyone will know the man-god has appeared if they do not see him disappear. Perhaps man will be really free and really divine "when it doesn't make any difference whether you live or not." And only a God can be so indifferent. Therefore, if he Kirillov knowing what is at stake, kills himself, he becomes a god, whether he knows it or not, and "even against my will." If he knows that he is sovereign, then he is all the more "bound to assert his will in the highest point." But he admits that he is unhappy just because he is bound to prove his freedom. That is why Kirillov turns out to be "a reluctant God."

Kirillov is detached but afraid, afraid to kill himself and yet detached from self-interest. On the contrary, he would "save mankind," by showing them all the way of courage. The "courage to be" (Tillich) is for him the courage not to be. But to us this courage is foolishness. God will not be replaced by the man-god, but by a fool, whether his proper name is Kirillov or Verhovensky or Smerdyakov. And the fool who does not know he is a fool can be dangerous. Kirillov only kills himself, but he kills a man with a great soul, if not a great idea. And Verhovensky kills a much better man than himself, Shatov, who had passed beyond nihilism and become a believer and family man. Smerdyakov kills a sensualist and a bad father, but his own father. It is as if some men had all their humanity drained out of them, until all that was left was a bad brain good for making syllogisms. Even hate had been drained away. For where there is no love at all, even of the self, there can be no hate either.

Kirillov has no secret. No one is curious about what he will do next. And yet Stavroguin, who mystifies everyone, has much less to tell about himself. He has thought out all the alternatives, proposed each one to a different friend, and rejected them all. Unlike Kirillov, he is not enamored of his own ideas. When he listens to others, it is impatiently and even contemptuously. He is like a sacrificial figure in a tragedy, the leader of the chorus. He has dived deeper in lawlessness and chaos than anyone else. The others have memorized his lessons, each thinking he owns a part of Stavroguin. But Stavroguin knows that he is nobody. "From me nothing has come but negation, with no greatness of soul, no force. Even negation has not come from me. Everything has always been petty and spiritless. Kirillov, in the greatness of his soul could not compromise with an idea and shot himself, but I see that he was great souled because he had lost his reason. I can never lose my reason, and I can never believe in an idea to such a degree as he did. I can never shoot myself." Instead he hung himself.

He was wrong when he said that not even negation had come from him. He had ruined other people's lives, capriciously, to see whether by doing so he could take something seriously. And even near the end he could say, "I'm still capable of wishing to do something decent, but the next moment I want to do evil things." He became tormented by the nightmare of a child raising her fist against him. "Pity for her stabbed me, a maddening pity, and I would have given my body to be torn to pieces if that would have erased what had happened." Pity is the double's substitute for love. Pity gives nothing away; he who pities stands back from and does not share in the suffering of the victim. Stavroguin could not even imagine the suffering of the girl who told her mother, "I killed God." Only one who loves both purity and God would interchange them in this way. Stavroguin had never known either. If he is attractive to everyone, it is because he wants to be without shame. He is like a Houdini trying to break the ropes which are too strong for him to loosen. There is a magical quality about Stavroguin, the perverted integrity of a soul that hates deception and yet always mystifies others.

Stavroguin is to Kirillov as struggling is to decision, or experience to theory. Stavroguin is an authentic double, Kirillov a sham. Kirillov loves the image of the crucified, but cannot believe in a risen Christ. "Alexey Kirillov" may well have been intended to remind the learned of the great Cyril, Bishop of Alexandria, who condemned the Nestorians because they too did not believe the man Jesus Christ rose from the dead. Stavroguin, who needed to carry a cross, broke Bishop Tihon's crucifix, but absent-mindedly. Just so his own life came to nothing because his mind could not repose in itself. He had "never felt nostalgia for the past;" he believed "everything here is alien," that there is "no forgiveness for me." Like Camus' Meursault, in rejecting pity he snarled, "I want everyone to stare at me." And yet he accepted the body of Liza and selfishly insulted her soul, because he hoped she would break his self-isolation. "I knew I didn't love you . . . I had a hope, a last hope. . . . For a moment I believed it." But this did not involve God, only someone else almost as despairing as himself. A world without God offers no resting-place for those who are unwilling to carry crosses.

IVAN, THE UNQUIET JUDGE

Kirillov would save mankind from loneliness, Ivan from crime. These are the major consequences of the destruction of God. While not believing in God any more than Kirillov does, Ivan too loves the image of Christ. "The kiss of Christ glowed in his heart." When Ivan is asked by his father whether he believes in God and immortality, he says he does not. There is only "absolute nothingness." Nor does his Grand Inquisitor believe in God; in fact, that is his secret. When he tells Alyosha that he "accepts God," we notice that he says he accepts God without understanding Him. He accepts God but does not accept His world. He accepts God as one accepts a Euclidean postulate, but he cannot accept the reality to which the postulate should apply. Obviously the postulate has no significance. The only reality which he does accept is the reality that might satisfy his "unseemly thirst for life." "I have a longing for life, and I go on living in spite of logic. Though I may not believe in the order of the universe, yet I love the sticky little leaves as they open in spring. I love the blue sky, I love some people, whom one loves you know sometimes without knowing why . . . . It's not a matter of intellect or logic, it's loving with one's inside, with one's stomach." And when Alyosha asks him whether he means that one should "love life more than the meaning of it," he replies, "Certainly, love it, regardless of logic as you say . . . and it's only then one will understand the meaning of it."

Ivan's problem is not loving life or finding meaning. His problem is to be able to accept the world as it is right now. For in his universe there are three basic elements: no-God, human freedom, and crime. The first two are causes, the third their consequence. He feels he cannot live without justice, and yet he wants to live. He can see only rebellion as the lot of a man who hates injustice, and he knows that man cannot live with equanimity in rebellion. Since he will not even consider any other alternatives, he has to live in a brain-whirling agony.

He is without doubt the most intellectual of all Dostoevsky's characters, and yet, unlike Kirillov, is incapable of dying for an idea. Like Stavroguin he has too many ideas. He has a genius for asking all the right questions which call for answers which are never wholly satisfactory. There is no doubt that he sincerely loves life—although his passion for life sounds a little rhetorical—and he can be respected for his expressed love for children. But he loves them from a distance, through his reading of the newspapers. He loves children because reason tells him that an affront to them poses a test case for God or some advocate of God to solve. It is easy to forget that he is only twenty-three years old, still young enough to spend most of his time talking of the "eternal questions." He is not yet committed either to children or to the blue sky; in fact, they are only two of the many themes he plays with.

It would be a waste of time to doubt the sincerity of his pity for those he has not met. What needs explaining is why such a reserved and self-sufficient person should care at all about injustices. Is it because he resented his own fatherless childhood; could he resent injustice primarily because he felt he had been treated without parental affection? Did he wish for justice even more than for life, and for natural justice at that? Was he too proud to admit that he wanted this justice mainly to compensate himself? He confesses bitterly that every man hates his father. He suggests that there is no natural law to love anyone: no one had loved him. And yet he will not accept this conclusion as final either. On the one hand, he generalizes to suit himself; on the other hand, he cannot live with the alternatives which these generalizations lead to. In this way he is not just an intellectual, for he respects certain unexpressed premises even more than the conclusions suggested by experience.

Ivan idolizes logical order and individual freedom. He can only respect an order that is freely arrived at, and a freedom that brings arithmetical justice and order. This is what he has in mind when he uses the word "natural." His experience and his reading, however, indicate that nature is not quite like this, that men do not live in justice or love most of the time, and when they do, it is only because they are believing in an order that does not exist. "If you were to destroy in mankind the belief in immortality, not only love but every living force maintaining the life of the world would at once be dried up." God and immortality, the two eternities, had been destroyed, and the lake of life was drying up. The logical consequences can be read in the daily papers. "Nothing then would be immoral, everything would be lawful."

What then should a man believe? Kirillov felt that with God gone, man would have to live alone, if he lived at all. But Ivan went further, holding that if egoism is all that is left, then man should be willing to accept egoism and even crime "as the inevitable, the most rational, even honorable outcome of his position." And yet he could not accept either. He could not reconcile his knowledge of a world of egoism with his longing for a world without egoism. This is not the same as saying that Ivan is a God-seeker. And he never guesses that the very justice he desires might be divine justice. Having accepted that Jesus died once for all, he cannot think of God except as an abstraction. On the other hand, he cannot live with the abstraction of his own dilemma. He cannot achieve order at the expense of freedom, even though he knows "that most men prefer peace and even death to freedom of choice in the knowledge of good and evil . . . . Nothing is more seductive for man than his freedom of conscience, but nothing is a greater cause of suffering." Ivan is not willing to surrender his admiration of ideas in the face of their consequences which he shrinks from.

An outsider begins his revolt with contempt for mediocrity, but when society disintegrates to the point where lawlessness is more noticeable than mediocrity, the outsider attacks a new enemy, but for the same reason. We must admit that not every outsider may realize that rebellion and self-reliance are not the same as self-will. One self-will, one freedom, is turned in on self and ultimately destructive; the other is a guarantee against enslavement to others as well as to oneself. Whoever values autonomy above all else, will not care much for others. And whoever hates enslavement can understand that no order is valid unless it is freely achieved. Ivan Karamazov rejects the justice that brings enslavement with it, and that diminishes the autonomy as well. He also rejects self-will because he has seen that in a world without God it is self-will above all that has brought man to crime. Without justification of some sort, he argues, everything may be lawful. But he does not really think so; and because he cannot find any evidence of natural law, he does not know why he should not believe that egoism and crime are not perfectly respectable.

Ivan's thinking is, as I have said, conditional. He must try one hypothesis after another, one conclusion after another, until he has exhausted them all and himself. In a world without law and order, without God or immortality, egoism is all that is left unless man has an innate desire for law to which he can relate his love for freedom. Some men can embrace nihilism, just as others can embrace collectivism. If man is to be saved from despair, he can choose either, the way of the individual or the way of the group. Perhaps they will both come to the same end. "Nothing needs to be destroyed," if you are a nihilist. "We only need to destroy the idea of God in man . . . . As soon as men have all of them denied God, the old conception of the universe will fall of itself . . . and the old morality, and everything will begin anew. Men will unite to take from life all it can give, but only for joy and happiness in the present world. Man will be lifted up with a spirit of Titanic pride and the man-god will appear." This is a return to Raskolnikov's antithesis between ordinary and extraordinary men, except that a new definition of extraordinary is being given. It also anticipates Nietzsche's *The Joyful Wisdom*, written two years later.

The extraordinary man was the first to understand what was happening in the nineteenth century. As the century advanced he became gradually more concerned over the metaphysical vacuum than with his own autonomy. He who earlier would have gloried in the uniqueness of his intelligence and energy, now realizes that there is greater distinction in being one of the first to see that God is dead. In His absence all standards and values are cheapened, and only two broad alternatives remain: rebellion or suspense. Kirillov, Raskolnikov, and Nietzsche chose rebellion; Ivan looked at the future of rebellion and held back. "One can hardly live in rebellion, and I want to live." Rebellion imitates the nothingness that surrounds man without God, and freedom becomes a theatrical gesture. He even puts aside with contempt the delusion that "man will love his brother without need of reward," if he has destroyed the idea of God. God is dead, and without God man can do nothing to keep freedom free. The closest Ivan can come is to do nothing.

HOMELESSNESS

In Dostoevsky's mythology the maxim of nihilism is, "everything is lawful," and it is meant to replace love of God and love of neighbor. Even love of self vanishes. The Underground Man loves nobody. Raskolnikov's flaw of pity is the crack in his self-isolation. Ivan only talks of pity; he can love only an image. Kirillov too can only love the same image of Christ. Nietzsche, however, is bolder. His equivalent of "everything is lawful" is "a transvaluation of values." He too loved no one. As long as he thought more about ideas than about himself, he remained sane. When he desperately and foolishly asked his non-existent readers why he was so wise, so clever, and why he wrote such excellent books, he was near collapse. He had lived too long off ideas, and ideas are not enough. Having no capacity for love of others—and no nostalgia or contemplative power to nourish him—he had to fall back on an image which would summarize all his ideas, namely, himself. He is a perfect illustration of Dostoevsky's man without love.

In Dostoevsky's novels only Kirillov and Ivan talk about the death of God. Neither is a double manifesting affective or moral ambivalence, although both have the deeper ambivalance of longing and despair. Nietzsche is not a double at all, with the double's dilemma of repressed inwardness. The double is abnormal; he cannot accept the judgment of the infinite over him. And so he turns to himself, kicks over the traces of morality, and acts capriciously in any way that can demonstrate self-will. What Kierkegaard meant by the infinite, Dostoevsky put in terms of justice, order, law, love. When they are missing, man has two alternatives. He can exercise his self-will as a demonstration of his independence, or he can recognize the reason why he cannot choose good rather than evil. The double who does not fully understand his repression, substitutes caprice for the choice of the good that he no longer touches. The double who does fully understand his repression knows also that caprice is useless. And so instead of exercising his will foolishly, he exercises his intellect. The double who proclaims the death of God is a man of ideas rather than a man of self-will. Even Kirillov wills his self away. As he says, he has no higher idea than disbelief in God. Ivan does have a higher idea, the justice which he cannot identify with the justice of God; this idea is strong enough to keep him from killing himself.

Recognizing that God is dead will not release the double from his depression, any more than caprice will. The next step is to ask whether a man who is not a double will avoid the double's fate if he too knows that God is dead. Nietzsche was a man who skipped the stages of inwardness and doubleness; he knew consciousness only. He had no sense of justice, law, order, or love. He could see history illustrating self-will and lack of self-will, but little else. He had no experience of having humbled himself to anyone admirable or adorable. All his themes were introspective: will, power, memory, vision, identity. And because he had no sense of anyone more adorable than himself, he was not aware of any repression. Whether some instinct for love or justice was unconsciously repressed is a question we cannot get at. He was also without a sense of guilt or anxiety, except the anxiety that he be admired. Like Stendhal, Nietzsche saw that his environment was unfavorable to independent minds. Unlike Stendhal, he did not think of his time primarily in political and social terms. From the beginning he wanted recognition, not association, and his objections to his contemporaries speak of a world that cannot comprehend himself. In order to pay them back for their indifference Nietzsche tried to remove the props of their metaphysical comfort. If he could not hurt them very much, he might make his own solitude seem more heroic. He was not interested in saving mankind; he knew well that mankind would not care for his kind of salvation. He who understood the function of resentment in others, never saw how much resentment underlay his own will to power.

He also claimed to discern a deep pessimism beneath bourgeois optimism. Perhaps he was right. Perhaps the crowd, the herd, secretly feared that the old certitudes were being vaporized. Perhaps they did suspect that with God discredited all absolutes would lose their authority. And perhaps they were already quietly closing their minds to such a horror. How can we tell now? Nietzsche himself seems never to have felt the horror personally, enough to despair, as Dostoevsky's characters who chose death rather than to live in such a world.

Good Friday has never been a day of rejoicing, and it is called "good" only because the sacrifice made then was justified by the Resurrection. Nietzsche thought it good for the opposite reason, because there was no Resurrection, and he had no rival to contend with. He realized that weaker souls would feel homeless without God, without the "joyful wisdom" of his death. He himself never spoke of homesickness as something a man is right to feel. The most significant fact about Nietzsche is just this, that he had no homesickness for justice or persons. And above all, he was not nostalgic for God. He was that most curious of human types, one who could recognize homelessness without himself feeling homesick. The only symptom of being at home that he experienced was wanting to be recognized. He once said that those who have a God for company do not know what solitude is, and that he had neither friends nor a God. He never discovered that home is not only the place where one is recognized, but also the place where one recognizes others. In destroying the idea of the greatest recognizer of all, God, he destroyed recognition. In his ignorance he boasted that he and others like him might yet bequeath mankind a home.

THE END OF HISTORY

In 1881 Nietzsche spent the summer in the Engadine at Sils Maria. His health was exceptionally good. And yet out of this physical wellbeing came his two bleakest ideas: the death of God and the eternal recurrence. *The Joyful Wisdom* and *Thus Spake Zarathustra* were written soon after, and written around these two intuitions. They are the first books of his maturity. In paragraph 108 of the first book he says that just as after Buddha's death his shadow was shown in caves for centuries, so now that God is dead, his shadow will also be shown in caves. Like the men in chains in Plato's image of the cave, the pious will pine without knowledge, taking shadows for reality. Those who have seen the sun, like Zarathustra, may descend with their wisdom from Alpine eyries to re-educate the world. So Christians had once hid from persecution in the catacombs, decorating the cavernous walls with the symbols of their dead God. Now the churches are caves in which men hide from the busy world, with its fever of life, attending masquerades of an exploded holiness. "If I looked into a mirror and did not see my face, I should have the sort of feeling which actually comes upon me, when I look into this living, busy world, and see no reflexion of its Creator. Were it not for this voice, speaking so clearly in my conscience and my heart, I should be an atheist when I looked into the world" (J. H. Newman,

1864). Nietzsche, not having a voice in his conscience or heart, had no other way of knowing that God might not be dead.

The parable entitled "The Madman," paragraph 125 of *The Joyful Wisdom*, would by itself justify our calling Nietzsche great, as philosopher and as artist. If he had written nothing else, this would guarantee his being remembered. It is holy scripture for anyone who would try to understand the intellectual climate of the late nineteenth and twentieth centuries. For once his irony is implied rather than stated, and the narrative is completely at the service of the philosophical critique, which itself is implied by the narrative.

The Madman: Have you ever heard of the madman who on a bright morning lighted a lantern and ran to the marketplace calling out unceasingly: "I seek God! I seek God!" As there were many people standing about who did not believe in God, he caused a great deal of amusement. "Why! is he lost?" said one. "Has he strayed away like a child?" said another. "Or does he keep himself hidden? Is he afraid of us? Has he taken a sea-voyage? Has he emigrated?" the people cried out laughingly. The insane man jumped into their midst and transfixed them with his glances. "Where is God gone?" he called out. "I mean to tell you! *We have killed him,* you and I! We are all murderers! But how have we done it? How were we able to drink up the sea? Who gave us the sponge to wipe away the whole horizon? What did we do when we loosened this earth from its sun? Whither does it now move? Whither do we move? Away from all suns? Do we not dash on unceasingly? Backwards, sideways, forwards, in all directions? Is there still an above and below? Do we not stray, as through infinite nothingness? Does not empty space breathe upon us? Has it not become colder? Does not night come on continually, darker and darker? Shall we not have to light lanterns in the morning? Do we not hear the noise of the grave-diggers who are burying God? Do we not smell the divine putrefaction?—for even gods putrefy! *God is dead!* God remains dead! And we have killed him? How shall we console ourselves, the most murderous of all murderers? The holiest and the mightiest that the world has hitherto possessed, has bled to death under our knife. Who will wipe the blood from us? With what water could we cleanse ourselves?

What lustrums, what sacred games shall we have to devise? Is not the magnitude of this deed too great for us? Shall we not ourselves have to become gods, merely to seem worthy of it? There never was a greater event. And on account of it all who are born after us belong to a higher history than any history hitherto!" Here the madman was silent and looked again at his hearers; they also were silent and looked at him in surprise. At last he threw his lantern on the ground, so that it broke in pieces and was extinguished. "I come too early," he said, "I am not yet at the right time. This prodigious event is still on its way, and is travelling; it has not yet reached men's ears. Lightning and thunder need time, the light of the stars needs time, deeds need time, even after they are done, to be seen and heard. This deed is as yet further from them than the furthest star. And yet they have done it!" It is further stated that the madman made his way into different churches on the same day, and there intoned his *Requiem aeternam deo.* When led out and called to account, he always gave the reply: "What are these churches now, if they are not tombs and monuments of God?"

The madman was Nietzsche himself, frenzied, incoherent, incomprehensible to the sane people, insane in reality for eleven years. Only a madman could speak the terrible truth in the open. And he could speak in safety because his hearers were too far from belief to know what he was talking about. They mocked God, not he. He, with pretended passion, sought a God who was so meaningless that He could be mocked without fear of blasphemy. The pretense is dropped, and the irony changes into an aggressive didacticism. "I mean to tell you. We have killed him." And again we hear the pronoun "we." *We* are responsible, *we* cannot get out of it. *We* did it. *We* are in this together. The enormity of it, the sea, the horizon, the earth, the sun, motions, directions, all changed, utterly changed. We are wanderers, and all around us is "infinite nothingness." The Pascalian empty spaces, cold, dark, requiring lanterns even in the morning. The day is dawning, the morning red with blood, and the corpse in the garden rotting. Who are the gravediggers? The pious, the clergy, anyone who has forgotten what it means to be a Christian, as Kierkegaard put it? Or are *we* the murderers, all of us, elected

as gravediggers? "God is dead," and will remain dead. This is final,
there will be no resurrection. But *we*, how daring, how heroic, pale
criminals laden down with a crime so great, so holy that we are
pariahs unless we can find new rituals of purification. The crime was
so great, too great, that we must become worthy of it by replacing
the man we have killed. Like Kirillov we dream of becoming gods.
For this is the greatest event of history; it is the end of history as we
have known it up to this point. God represented another world,
invisible, unprovable, comforting and poisonous. It never existed
except in our minds; we must be strong enough to get along without
it. But we must first understand, and nobody does understand. It's
too soon. Later on they will know what *they* have already done.
We are not *they* any more; for *we* know and *they* do not. Now a
sad irony returns as the madman—as Nietzsche—finishes within the
empty church the requiem to the dead god. The church is a tomb, a
monument—why not a theater too (Kierkegaard)—empty, not because the god has risen but because there has never been a god at
all, not to believe in, not to kill, and not to bury. It has been just a
game all along.

The madman—the same Nietzsche—may not have been seeking
God, but he was definitely seeking someone else who could understand that there is no God to seek. The absolutes are gone, the transcendental worlds of idea, value, person, and paradise. The only
question is how long it will take everyone to miss them. Men cling
to formulas, all the more defensively as the darkness of infinite
nothingness closes in. As his contemporaries clung, largely indifferent to the darkness, his exasperation at their indifference rose to
anger, and he tried to shock them into some awakening. "Have
you understood me? Dionysos versus Christ?" But how could they
understand either the blasphemy or his own resentment of Christ if
they had long ceased to understand Christ? Kierkegaard could have
told him that.

Later on, in paragraph 343 of the same book he repeats his conviction that he is living at the turning point of history, after "the most
important of recent events, that God is dead." Again he speaks of
the shadows cast over Europe as "our entire European morality"
crumbles, and as more and more people suspect that "belief in the

Christian God has become unworthy of belief." But the event is still "far too great, too remote, too much beyond people's power of apprehension." Who has understood it well enough to be the "teacher and herald of such a tremendous logic of terror, prophet of a period of gloom and eclipse the like of which has probably never taken place on earth before?" Who but himself, and Dostoevsky? The very pillars of civilization were falling down one by one, Truth, Morality, God. Each had contributed to a stability which life otherwise would not have, each had protected man from metaphysical and psychological insecurity. Nietzsche welcomed the insecurity because he said it would force men to depend on their own energies.

But for a while the effects of this great event will be bewildering. As he explains in paragraph 285 man will no longer be able to pray or worship or trust; he will be alone in his seven solitudes. And even those like himself who have no genuine sympathy for "this period of gloom" will lose confidence and courage; their world "must seem to them daily more darksome, distrustful, strange, and old." And yet at the same time as "premature children of the coming century" they will begin to see that the long term effects are "rather like a new and indescribable variety of light, happiness, relief, enlivenment, encouragement, and dawning day." And then follows (paragraph 343) one of the more euphoristic passages. "Our hearts overflow with gratitude, astonishment, presentiment, and expectation. At last the horizon seems open once more, granting even that it is not bright . . . the sea, *our* sea, again lies open before us; perhaps never before did such an 'open sea' exist." Perhaps not, and it is equally unlikely that ever before there had been such rejoicing over a dead god—except, of course, in the fictitious mind of Ivan Karamazov, who said, "Man will feel such lofty joy that it will make up for all his old dreams of the joys of heaven."

THE REAL *PRIMUM MOBILE*

The sage Zarathustra, just down from a mountain top, met a saint in a forest who had not heard that God is dead. He met also the last pope, who said that he had been present when God died: "He suffocated of his all-too-great pity." God had seen "how *man* hung on the cross, and could not endure it." Whether God suffocated of pity or was murdered matters little. "Away with such a God! Better have no God, better to set up destiny on one's own account, better to be a fool, better to be God oneself!" Better no doubt to be a Kirillov or a Nietzsche. Better to be someone like "the ugliest man" who murdered God because "he beheld men's depths and dregs, all his hidden ignominy and ugliness. His pity knew no modesty; he crept into my dirtiest corners. This most prying, over-intrusive, over-pitiful one had to die. He never beheld *me;* on such a witness I would have revenge—or not live myself. The God who beheld everything, and also man, that God had to die. Man cannot endure it that such a witness should live." It is such a passage as this which has encouraged commentators to speak of Nietzsche's personal resentment against religion, and his motive of revenge. He himself had asked why anyone should want revenge if he does not despise himself as much as he loves himself. Otherwise he could accept pity. Man is, therefore, "something that has to be surpassed."

Nietzsche enjoyed tolling the requiem bell. The grief and alarm that others might hear was a resurrection hymn for that eager sexton. Man has arisen; Dionysos lives once more. His enthusiasm may have been premature, but it seems genuine. In passage after passage his savage anti-Christian bias leaves no doubt where he stood. "Life is at an end where the kingdom of God begins." "God is a conjecture . . . such an obvious and crass solution." "I regard Christianity as the most fatal and seductive lie that has ever yet existed." "One should take no rest until this thing is utterly destroyed." "The time is coming when we shall have to pay for having been Christians for two thousand years." And so he rejected this "Platonism of the people," a supra-sensible order which had given civilized men "the equilibrium which enables us to live," and tried to substitute the subjectivism which Dostoevsky called Titanism. He could accept nihilism with all its consequences because he really believed that man had the power to do what God alone had been supposed to have done, create, make something from nothing. The artist brings into being that which was not there before him; the philosopher sets new goals and establishes new values. The artist-philosopher comes as close to creation, in the literal sense, as anyone can. Had he not already created God, and then found him in his way?

Man wants "a world that does not contradict itself, that does not deceive, that does not change, a world in which there is no suffering." Such a world must exist because it ought to exist; it ought to exist because man needs it. And so man invents the concept of truth in order to provide intellectual and emotional stability, and the concept of Being in order to confirm the reliability of truth. "The real *primum mobile* is the Disbelief in Becoming." The world of becoming is the world of change and suffering. If a man cannot accept suffering, he can invent Being and Truth so that he can tell himself that change and suffering are only accidental and temporary. Woe to that man when he can no longer convince himself that Being lurks behind Becoming, waiting for the right time to confirm that all things are well.

Nietzsche's highest idea, his real *primum mobile*, is his own disbelief and scorn of Being. And *we* "have a picture of a creature who would not require the belief in Being." It is easy to understand his scorn for those who have deceived themselves, if they have; it is harder to understand or sympathize with his scorn for the need and desire of Being. It is one thing to reject what you yourself have had no part in making, it is another to resent the very concept of stability. Can stability be disposed of simply by suggesting that its very notion is a product of historical development or psychological need? This question does not bear its answer within it, of course, but neither does the contrary suggestion. Nietzsche thought he was refuting God in the name of human self-sufficiency. Where had he experienced self-sufficiency except in his own desiring? In rejecting God he also rejected—at least in intention—the assumption that "the axioms of logic are adequate to reality." He was one of the first, to be sure, to say that the axioms of logic are only "measures and means by which alone we can create realities or the concept of reality." What kind of logic would be adequate for a concept of reality that accepted becoming, and suffering, as the only reality? How reliable would it be—or would one have to despair of reliability altogether? Nietzsche was always excessively sure he was right.

Nietzsche was not always consistent. On the one hand, he was certain that truth must be made, not found; invented, not discovered. On the other hand, he was equally sure that the existing world had an "essence," namely finite becoming. To be consistent with the first conviction he would have had to agree with Wittgenstein's dictum that "The sense of the world must lie outside the world. In the world everything is as it is and happens as it does happen. In it there is no value—and if there were it would be of no value. If there is a value which is of value, it must lie outside all happening and being-so." This agrees with his reading of the evidence, although it does not agree with his confidence that there is no value outside the world either. He confused suspicion sometimes with evidence, and for a negative proposition of existence there is no evidence.

In a sense he was right in thinking of himself as a disciple of Dionysos rather than of Prometheus, for Prometheus was not only defiant, he was gifted with foresight. And unlike Prometheus he was never to be released from suffering. He experienced nihilism at every level. He was present at God's death, but there was no God to die. He killed him, but there was no God to kill. He saw a world without meaning, and he lost his own mind before he could create new meaning. The only meaning he had to offer was the mind he had lost. He anticipated the conclusion when he cried, "Oh grant madness, you heavenly powers, madness that at last I may believe in myself. I am consumed by doubts, for I have killed the Law. If I am not more than the Law, then I am the most abject of all." His presumption may deserve no pity; no one can tell for sure whether it followed or preceded his thorough destruction of absolutes. But a vacuum, however achieved, must be filled. He knew that he had to "create something new." But what? In the end his honesty, his noblest virtue, forced him to admit, "I am falling to pieces, but I no longer care."

CHAPTER 6

The Great Noon

"We have produced the hardest possible thought—now let us create the creature who will accept it light-heartedly and blissfully."—Nietzsche

"New man, new life, a new everything."—Dostoevsky

NEITHER DOSTOEVSKY NOR NIETZSCHE accepted the death of God as the last word of history. As Good Friday is followed by the Resurrection, so the death of the God-man is succeeded by the rising of the man-god. History could begin again, with a new man or a new delusion. Nietzsche welcomed the age he would not witness, prophesying that out of a new barbarism could still come a new renaissance. Dostoevsky feared rather that the new man would be demonic and destructive, and that only moral regeneration could reverse the runaway flight to self-isolation.

However differently expressed, Dostoevsky and Nietzsche were envisioning the same future: regeneration, resurrection, return; new life, new law, new men, new barbarians, supermen. The differences are significant. Nietzsche's regeneration is something remembered, it is a return to what has already taken place many times. It is, therefore, physical and metaphysical, not moral. Dostoevsky's regeneration is moral rebirth, and can happen only in the future. Both writers speak of a new race of men who will arise in the twentieth century, after the death of God, and who will conquer the earth. These are the supermen (Nietzsche) or Titans (Dostoevsky), heralded with satisfaction by Nietzsche, imagined more ironically by Dostoevsky. They do not differ essentially from the select few, the free spirits already springing up here and there in the nineteenth century, except that they will not be as lonely, nor as distracted by

85

polemics with their duller contemporaries. Those born in an age of global war will not have to guard as carefully against the infectious bourgeois sicknesses of will and belief. All their energies will have been liberated for conquest and reconstruction.

While the Nietzschean heroes of Dostoevsky's novels who have rejected God and immortality have only self-will or no-will left to substitute for what they have lost, Nietzsche himself substituted will to power for God, and eternal recurrence for immortality. One might have expected Dostoevsky to try to restore God and immortality in some way. In fact, Dostoevsky was preoccupied with two quite different considerations: crime and resurrection. The crime of those who are involved in the death of God can only be expiated by regeneration, by the old man dying and a new birth. To what extent this rebirth involves God and immortality is another question.

The man who enters the dark night of God's death has very little chance of being reborn. That which Dostoevsky outlines ironically, even mockingly, Nietzsche proclaims with dramatic jubilation. Dostoevsky trusted only the regeneration that follows the death of self-willed man. There are, therefore, two kinds of regeneration: that which follows the death of God, and that which follows the death of self-isolation; and two kinds of new men; those who will be born at a later time, and those who can be reborn through suffering and purification at any time. Nietzsche had in mind a cultural regeneration, Dostoevsky an individual regeneration. In addition, Nietzsche looked towards a return of both the individual and his environment aeons later at the end of some cycle, while Dostoevsky expected the resurrection of the personality in a new body. Nietzschean eternal recurrence is not eternal life, but a substitute which conceivably might satisfy something in man that desired or needed eternity.

Only when history or personal existence reaches a dead end does regeneration look appealing, except, of course, to those who are so weary of life that they have no other wish but for extinction of fatigue or pain. And even then it will not appeal if the individual remembers a happy life, or at least happy moments. "The happy few" do not need a completely new life; they only need more of what they have already enjoyed. With no overwhelming regrets, indiffer-

ent to the realm of guilt and sin, they never experience a final deso-
lation. Minor heartaches and the disillusions of growing old and
unwanted can be brightened by art, scenery, and revery.

To both Dostoevsky and Nietzsche the time of the apocalypse was
approaching, the seven seals would be broken, and a new hell on
earth would be revealed. Alongside their prophecies Stendhal's private concerns seem as trivial as they are harmlessly charming. But
Kierkegaard, so serious that his very name now suggests seriousness,
had little apocalyptic sense and thought of the twentieth century only
as the time when he would be read and understood. Anticipator of a
theology of crisis, he had nothing to say about a civilization in crisis or
the new men that crisis would breed. Even more interesting to us now
is that this man who said he had written about Christianity so that
anyone reading him could find his way about in it, has nothing much
to say about the Resurrection, the kingpin of Christianity. He
wrote eloquently about love and faith; he was curiously silent about
hope.

Indeed Kierkegaard's definition of what it means to be a Christian
often seems to be limited to a suffering martyrdom, an ideal that he
found attractive because it fitted the self-imposed isolation of himself from loved ones and from God. He could not afford to give hope
a place in his thoughts unless he was willing to give it a place in his
life. From his younger days on he had thought of life solemnly as a
task to seek and to see through. But burdened by melancholy, guilt,
or some other temperamental inability to get out of himself, he came
more and more to assume that his tasks, the only tasks worthy to be
his, must be impossible. And although he knew well that with God
all things are possible, he rigidly separated the things that belong to
God and the things that belonged to himself. We may speculate now,
from a less lonely and better informed theological climate, that his
solitude should be understood as inevitable to anyone who, through
no fault of his own, is cut off from the living society of Christ, the
Catholic body of Christ. Even Kierkegaard came to suspect his local
Protestantism of having cut itself off from the main trunk of the tree
so that its life and doctrine were no longer recognizably Christian.
The body of Christ which Kierkegaard was acquainted with was for

all practical purposes a corpse, and the only recourse he had was communion with the invisible church. That is not good enough, for the living body is also the apostolic teacher without whom the truth is partial and exaggerated.

His death was as moving and ambiguous as his life. When asked whether he would like to receive Holy Communion, he replied, "Yes, but not from a parson, from a layman." Official Christendom had rejected the suffering Christ; he in his own sufferings would reject them. He would not compromise. And yet among his last words he wished to be remembered "to everyone. I was much attached to them all, and tell them my life was a great and to others unknown and unintelligible suffering. It all looked like pride and vanity, but it was not. I am no better than others." And so he was able to pray "that my sins be forgiven me, that everything be forgiven . . . that I may be free from despair in death." A little later he imagined himself sitting astride a cloud singing the angelic and resurrection word, "Alleluia! Alleluia! Alleluia!" It is no wonder that his niece seeing him in the hospital should have "seen the spirit break through its earthly frame . . . and lend it such brilliance, as though it were the glorified body at the dawn of the resurrection."

He had accomplished his task, although he knew a dead man would be listened to more intently than an alive one. His task had not been light, nor had it been simple. For the moment he seemed to have failed no one, not even his deathbed friend Emil Boesen understood him. They were all concerned about the scandal of his defiance of the church. But this seemed unimportant now to him, as he neared eternity and thought of the burden the Gospel itself imposed. He had said before, and he felt still, "I understand more and more that Christianity is really too holy for us men. Only think what it means to dare to believe that God came into the world, and for my sake too." He had never got used to the shock of the Incarnational Paradox, and the discovery that apparently no one else realized how improbable this reality was. If anyone after St. Athanasius could be called prophet of the Incarnation, it would be Kierkegaard. The contemplative side of his nature mused on and on over the event that Meister Eckhart's gloss on "thine almighty word leaped down from heaven and came to me" considered. That God should come to *me*—that was the great and mighty wonder. And that no one but Kierkegaard in Copenhagen should be amazed, that was bewildering. But that one thousand priests and bishops should complacently earn a living as that same Lord's officials, that was scandalous.

A lesser man could have been satisfied with this superiority to his fellows; Kierkegaard was miserable. For one thing he genuinely wanted others to know what he knew. For another, he realized that if God had come down to earth even for him, then he should be able to accept his presence and his mercy. "It was a miracle when Christ said to the paralytic, 'Thy sins are forgiven thee, arise and walk.' But if this miracle does not happen to me now, what a miraculous boldness of faith is involved in believing that the sin is entirely forgotten, so that the memory of it has no anguish, in believing that one has become a new man so that one can hardly recognize oneself again." It is not clear, however, that even on his deathbed he had become this new man. Years before he had said that "To wish to break down my self-isolation by continually thinking of breaking it down leads to the directly opposite result." But to the end he was suspicious of the overtures of others—probably justly—and intent still on justifying his lonely career.

With reason and with eloquence he had written about the sickness unto death, about the man who despairs "because he cannot get rid of himself." How well he knew this from the inside: "the need of solitude, which for him is a vital necessity, sometimes like breathing"; "the loss of the eternal and oneself"; "the restless spirit"; "the being offended at the whole of existence"; "the inwardness with a jammed lock"; "the demoniac shrewdness to keep despair shut up in close reserve." And yet he believed that somewhere in the depths of despair was a "passageway to the eternal." But first he must die to himself: *perissem nisi perissem*. If only he could! If only he did not have to suffer for the doctrine, if only he did not have to think so much about his role as poet and teacher of the doctrine of Christ! He would have preferred, I am sure, to be a "knight of the hidden inwardness." That is, one part of him would have preferred this. But I can never leave him without feeling that there is another and even more hidden inwardness which had nothing to do with faith, and which he himself may not have penetrated.

THE RETURN OF DIONYSOS

Far from wanting to break out of his self-isolation Nietzsche made it his principle of life and regeneration. He said he loved his fate (*amor fati*)—did he mean that he would try to love his fate? He called himself "the last disciple of the philosopher Dionysos—the teacher of the Eternal Return." From *The Birth of Tragedy* to *Ecce Homo* he identified himself with the Dionysian myth. "Have you understood me, Dionysos versus Christ?" Why Dionysos and not Christ? Why prefer a myth-god cut to pieces, to a real man hung on a cross? "God on the cross is a curse upon life, a signpost directing people to deliver themselves from it. Dionysos cut into pieces is a promise of life: it will be forever born anew, and rise afresh from destruction." He might just as well have interchanged the names; Dionysian rites were also meant to deliver men from suffering, and Christ's resurrection was meant to be the beginning of a new life. Perhaps the advantage that Christ had over Dionysos in actually having lived was precisely the reason why Nietzsche so resented him.

Nietzsche could not bear to think that any historical person had preceded him as a savior. Dionysos was only an idea which he himself would give reality to. Dionysos meant to him the ever shifting finite energy of the universe, dying and coming to life again. Dionysos means power, over-fullness, pain, suffering, joy, life, death, in fact everything. Dionysos means the seasons, nature, procreation, passion. Dionysos is the "substratum of the world . . . a monster of energy, without beginning or end which eternally regenerates itself." And this energy is will to power. In Nietzsche's mind Christianity is utterly opposed to this superabundant energy. He thought that Christ had not come to encourage mankind to be energetic, but to save them from the consequences of too much will and energy.

No doubt the Protestant Christendom he and Kierkegaard knew as Christianity was so conditioned by European bourgeois caution that it was almost impossible to imagine a Christ that had come to set men free. At no time, however, would Nietzsche have encountered a Christianity that did not soberly fear the consequences of unbridled self-will.

To extend the mythical symbolism a little, we might see will to power as Promethean, eternal return as Dionysian. And if we follow Nietzsche's scholastic terminology and say that "the innermost essence of existence is the will to power," we would wish to say that at the heart of Dionysos is Prometheus. The raw energy, the nuclear energy of the universe is defiance, and this is found over and over, in every conceivable pattern, and these patterns also are found over and over. If the existence can be spoken of apart from its essence, Nietzsche would have called it eternal recurrence. It was not until 1881, nine years after *The Birth of Tragedy,* that he came to think of eternal recurrence as a separate metaphysical principle. And only then did he distinguish will to power from eternal recurrence as essence from existence. Later still he spoke of impressing on becom- ,ing the character of being, as he began to suppose that energy is recurrent and that each moment of defiance returns. And in spite of his affected detesting of the concept of being, he inconsistently hoped that individuals could stabilize the world of becoming: "Let us stamp the impress of eternity upon our lives."

It is as if Nietzsche was born with a feeling for will to power, and only along life's way discovered he needed eternal recurrence. Per- haps the will to power is the secret of any outsider, his autono- mous energy, his inspiration, his Promethean defiance. If there is a specifically Nietzschean problem the question is not *what* he needed the concept of will to power for, but *why* he felt he needed the con- cept of eternal recurrence. Having rejected all conventions, he re- jected also a rational order that treated purpose and unity as basic principles of reality. Nietzsche was certain that no matter what men said or thought, purposes are made by them, not found. When they do not know they have made them, they have in fact imagined them. It comes to the same thing, except that some men know what they are doing, and some deceive themselves and others. He himself preferred a world of sheer becoming, at any price, to a kind of stability that is always on the point of dwarfing the individual. He felt a personal affront, as it were, at the idea of a being who creates man and to whom man owes his life and freedom. Unlike Ivan Karamazov he was only too willing to live as a rebel. His own ideal was individual creativity without creation, or more exactly, inspiration and ecstasy without birth. It is possible—in the absence of an explanation by Nietzsche himself—that after a decade or more of trying to live in rebellion, he too, like the old God became too tired to live. It is easy to reject teleology, and not so easy to will just for the sake of willing.

Egoism can be frighteningly empty and fatiguing. Nietzsche's recurrent states of depression may have suggested to him that he find some justification for living apart from will to power. To put it in the scholastic terminology he himself fell back on, even an essence must have an existence, or be nothing at all. We need such an explanation to account for his vision beside Lake Silvaplana in the summer of 1881. Of this he said, "I was possessed by a new vision which I am the first man to know . . . the highest formula of affirmation that can ever be attained." Until then he had only the concept of will to power, and that had not proved to be enough. With characteristic lack of modesty he owned that "the doctrine of the eternal recurrence is the turning-point of history." For him, at least, it became a fortunate intuition useful for distracting him from the tiring efforts to feel exceptional. But although his will to power is a static notion, he probably hoped that repetition might confirm its vitality. Repetition may be a poor substitute for novelty, but in a mind that was exceptionally indifferent to novelty, repetition would have to serve. It did not seem to matter that the same things, and ideas, were to be willed again and again. Perhaps he found his security in repetition, especially of the two or three key ideas that run through his writings: death of God, will to power, eternal return. He never showed signs of wondering, hoping, even fearing that he might meet someone or something unexpectedly. Lacking the anticipatory sense of his mentor Stendhal, he carried his own world inside himself. He may have been aware of the difference when he said,

"Everything seems to me much too important to be so fleeting. I seek an eternity for everything." He was looking, maybe unconsciously, for a way to get out of the horizontal plane of a succession of acts of the will, a layer of existence where all things appear fleeting. Eternal recurrence may have been his way to save himself from his kind of boredom.

He meant what he said when he spoke of the concept of eternal recurrence as the gateway to the future. On one side of the gate the sign reads, "God is dead"; on the other it reads, "All things recur eternally." The philosopher who proclaimed God's death was also the first to know eternal recurrence—or so he believed. Looking to the past he saw a massive dependence on imagined absolutes, looking to the future he envisaged a race of new individuals beside whom he himself would be only a pale shadow. Whether disposed towards history or towards apocalypse, Nietzsche's critical sense must always be taken seriously. It is only when he shifts into the gear of self-appreciation that we become uneasy. "Such things have never been written, never been felt, never been suffered; such suffering can be borne only by a God, Dionysos." Such things should not have been written by him; and they are not true.

VERTICAL ETERNITY

Although Nietzsche never quite admitted it, he knew the dread of repetition and unrelieved succession. This can be seen in the passage where he first wrote of eternal recurrence (paragraph 341 of *The Joyful Wisdom*).

The Heaviest Burden: What if a demon crept after thee into thy loneliest loneliness some day or night, and said to thee: "This life as thou livest it at present and hast lived it, thou must live it once more, and also innumerable times; and there will be nothing new in it, but every pain and every joy and every thought and every sigh, and all the unspeakably small and great in thy life must come to thee again, and all in the same series and sequence—and similarly this spider and this moonlight among the trees, and similarly this moment, and I myself. The eternal sand-glass of existence will ever be turned once more, and thou with it, thou speck of dust!" Wouldst thou not throw thyself down and gnash thy teeth, and curse the demon that so spake? Or hast thou once experienced a tremendous moment in which thou wouldst answer him: "Thou art a God and never did I hear anything so divine!"

The same spider in the philosopher's bedroom, the same moonlight in the trees outside the window as he sits at his writing table, a veritable vertical eternity. Of course it would be boring, a burden to consider, madness to have to carry. But it might yet be saved by "a tremendous moment." Everything depends on that. "We must not strive after distant and unknown states of bliss and blessings and acts of grace, but we must live so that we would fain live again and live forever so, to all eternity!" Did Nietzsche remember having experienced such moments? Did he have the power, and was there time, to experience others? What is involved is what he called inspiration. A passage in *Ecce Homo* describes with an explicitness unusual with Nietzsche.

> Something profoundly convulsive and disturbing suddenly becomes visible and audible with indescribable definiteness and exactness. One hears—one does not seek; one takes—one does not ask who gives: a thought flashes out like lightning . . . there is an ecstasy whose terrific tension is sometimes released by a flood of tears, during which one's progress varies from involuntary impetuosity to involuntary slowness. There is a feeling that one is utterly out of hand, with the most distinct consciousness of an infinitude of shuddering thrills that pass through one from head to foot—there is a profound happiness in which the most painful and gloomy feelings are not discordant in effect, but are required as necessary colors in this overflow of light.

The authenticity of his experience of ecstasy need not be doubted if we still ask whether this is not inspiration without content, static creativity. And it is fair to use Nietzsche's own rhetorical logic on him and ask which kind of inspiration and ecstasy is superior, with or without content? Apparently he did not think to ask.

Can we live again? His answer comes with an admirable simplicity: "We do live again." He has no proof, no evidence, only a little allegory of a gateway and a spider in the moonlight.

> There was a gateway just where we halted. Look at this gateway. It hath two faces. Two roads come together here: these hath no one yet gone to the end of. This long lane backwards; it continueth for an eternity. And that long lane forward—that is another eternity. They are antithetical to one another, these roads, and it is here at this gateway that they come together. The name of this gateway is inscribed above: "This Moment."

> Observe, This Moment! From the gateway, This Moment, there runneth a long eternal lane backwards, behind us lieth an eternity. Must not whatever *can* run its course of all things, have already run along that lane? Must not whatever *can* happen of all things have already happened? And if everything has already existed, what thinkest thou of This Moment? Must not this gateway also have already existed? And this slow spider which creepeth in the moonlight, and this moonlight itself, and thou and I in this gateway whispering together, whispering of eternal things—must we not all have already existed? And must we not return and run in that other lane out before us, that long weird lane, must we not eternally return?

If the "thou" was a real person, possibly Lou Salome with whom he had had long conversations before he wrote *Thus Spake Zarathustra*, from which this passage is taken, then This Moment was memorable enough to record and crystallize. But the air is heavy and the heart already weary from the contemplation of horizontal eternity. To be redeemed from its tedium his mind imagined the same eternity in depth, like a block of ice, infinite in length, and infinite in depth. Each moment is embedded forever and reflects all the other similar moments of past and future. The way is open now to become indifferent to time altogether.

Nietzsche's cosmology and physics were certainly not original; they themselves have recurred throughout the history of ideas. He wrote that "this universe is a monster of energy, a finite and brazen quantity of energy which grows neither bigger nor smaller. . . . The energy of the universe can only have a given number of possible qualities . . . the activity is eternal." He offers no proof; it is a theory that fits his needs. He needs to rescue some fine moments from the anonymity of the overwhelming remainder. He dreamed that such great moments had not vanished irrevocably into the obscurity of nothingness but would return many times and be enjoyed all over. He dreamed, he hoped, he believed, and he affirmed. It became his creed. "The middle is everywhere," and he stood everywhere, and in the middle.

Even so it is natural to wonder how this philosopher of history could so easily brush aside the passage of time, especially his own death. He had thought of this too, and he replied to himself that between the "last moment of consciousness and the first ray of the dawn of your new life no time will elapse, as a flash of lightning will the space go by, even though living creatures think it is billions of years. Timelessness and immediate re-birth are compatible once intellect is eliminated." Why then care about time; time cannot care about the dead. His answer does not quite answer the dread of nothingness in the heart of the living. Perhaps the philosopher was so engaged in thought that he had forgotten the threat to his own being. Otherwise he might not have regarded non-existence as compatible with existence.

Eternal recurrence soon became "the great disciplinary thought" to save and justify his *taedium vitae*. Inspired at noon in an Alpine sun, hot, blinding, shadowless, he was illuminated by light, heat, energy and saw in them the stuff of the universe, the life of his mind. He said that he felt, "I have been here before. I have thought this before. I have dreamed this before." And he probably had. It is not difficult to see how he could be satisfied with it, difficult so long as we think of ourselves and not of a man who was convinced he was unique. "In every one of these cycles of human life, there will be one hour where for the first time one man, and then many, will perceive the mighty thought of the eternal recurrence of all things, and for mankind this is always the hour of *noon*." He was that one man, and he was determined to try to live the rest of his life so that there would be no night.

But first time must be stopped in the glare of some great moment experienced at high noon. And then the rest of life must be made to reverberate with the memory of this moment. Like Kirillov, Nietzsche had a "great idea," great because it would make him great, as great as a god. He said that "Schopenhauer did not understand how to deify this will . . . . He did not realize that there is an infinite number of ways of being different, and even of being God." His own fate was to be, as he wished, a complete outsider, as alien as a god. He had withdrawn in shyness, then observed with contempt and sarcasm; his critique of history is one long drawn out diatribe. He called all absolutes a swindle, he found the very idea of God crass. He rejected the security of a divine order, and yet divinized the worn out conception of a "deep, deep eternity." Anything, even repetition, can make a man happy, if he wills it intensely enough. A man can become Prometheus if he is already Dionysos. A man ought to be able by standing still and glaring fixedly down into the ground of This Moment to forget time and boredom. Nietzsche tried. There is no evidence that he succeeded. He was still staring fixedly at the close.

We try to understand why a man should shut himself away from the possibility that there may be another kind of eternity than eternal recurrence, and we recall Kierkegaard's theory (in *Sickness unto Death*): "He is afraid of eternity—for the reason that it might rid him of his advantage over other men. He rages most of all at the thought that eternity might get it into its head to take his misery from him; rather than seek help he would prefer to be himself—with all the tortures of hell—if so it must be." The defiant despair of Nietzsche, "willing to be himself" may have become fused, in life-weariness, in a personality unwilling any longer to be itself, sitting behind "that blind door." As Kierkegaard went on to explain, "That blind door behind which there was nothing is in this case a real door, a door carefully locked, and behind it sits, as it were, the self and watches itself employed in filling up the time with not willing to be itself, and yet is self enough to love itself." But there the analogy breaks down; Nietzsche in the end could not even love himself.

TRANSFORMATIONS

Philosophically considered, Nietzsche's will to believe in eternal recurrence has an equivalent in Dostoevsky's epileptic visions. Even the language is similar. "There are moments and time suddenly stands still, and it will become eternal" (Kirillov). But Dostoevsky's moments actually did recur as by-products of his sickness, and his descriptions are more matter of fact and explicit than Nietzsche's.

> There are moments when all the intellectual and spiritual faculties, morbidly overstrained as it were, suddenly flare up in a bright flame of consciousness; and at such an instant the troubled soul, as though languishing with a foreboding of the future, with a foretaste of it, has something like a prophetic vision. And your whole being so longs for life, so begs for life; and aflame with the most burning, blindest hope, your heart seems to summon the future with all its mystery, with all its uncertainty, even with its storms and unheavals if only it brings life. (Prince Myshkin)

This is the sense of life just preceding the epileptic fit. "For this moment one might give one's whole life." He always associated each return of this moment with his memory of a scene on a parade ground in Moscow where he had heard the sentence of death read out and knew then that he had only a few minutes more to live. His epileptic history also began that day. Sentenced and reprieved—this was to be the recurrent pattern of his life. "Only a sentence of death distinguishes a man," Stendhal had said. And Dostoevsky would have added, only a sentence of death makes a man appreciate life, and a reprieve introduces a man to eternity.

He wrote *The Idiot* to show the effect such an experience would have, how it could transform and transfigure. Prince Myshkin is not like other men; he is like a visitor from a paradisal world. He is shrewd and yet so essentially trusting that he is called an "idiot." He himself knows that he lives on the dial's point; at any moment the strain of intuition may be too much and he will become an idiot in actuality. But "what does it matter, if the minute turns out to be the acme of harmony and beauty, of completeness, or proportion, or reconciliation, and of ecstatic devotional merging in the highest synthesis of life?" It does not matter perhaps, but it also is generally irrelevant to the greater number of human beings who are not given to visions, epileptic or other. And Dostoevsky knew this. Unlike Nietzsche he did not exclude other transformations out of fondness for his own peculiar condition.

However important to himself the ecstatic moment, Dostoevsky did not assume that it was the only way open to the isolated man or even the best way. He knew, of course, that most men are not epileptics; he was grateful that out of his disease should at least have come one benefit for himself. But the self-isolated characters of his novels are not epileptics, and whatever occasional visions of the supreme worth of life they may be granted, they have only a passing significance in their constant preoccupation with cosmic meaninglessness and personal isolation. No momentary vision, no matter how ecstatic, can make these problems vanish. They will suggest alternative solutions of their own, for Stavroguin one kind, for Ivan Karamazov another, for Raskolnikov a third, for Alyosha a fourth, and so on. But broken down into grand alternatives, there are essentially three: the nightmare vision of a new race of proud Titans, dreams of paradise, and moral and spiritual resurrection.

From *Crime and Punishment* to *The Brothers Karamazov* there is persistent preoccupation on Dostoevsky's part with a kind of man who runs the danger of not being able to break out of his self-isolation. Raskolnikov saw himself as one of the first of a race of extraordinary men who would ruin the world. Consciously he welcomed these new men; in his dreams he realized what their advent would mean.

The whole world was condemned to a terrible new strange plague that had come to Europe from the depths of Asia. . . . Never had men considered themselves so intellectual and so completely in possession of the truth as these sufferers . . . . Men killed each other in a sort of senseless spite . . . . The alarm bell was ringing all day long in the towns . . . . The plague spread . . . . Only a few men could be saved in the whole world. They were a pure chosen people, destined to found a new race and a new life, to renew and purify the earth, but no one had seen these men, no one had heard their words and their voices.

There is always a note of irony in Dostoevsky's accounts of the new men. He had no illusions. He pictures a world in which men are criminals because their reason says it is right to destroy. It is a world in which each man knows what is true, but where there is no truth except that which is imposed. In such a world theories and not men are the concerns of reason. It is also a world with the geography of the one we know—the plague comes from Asia, and once spread, the alarm bell will keep ringing all over Europe.

In one of these towns in European Russia the plague did come, the alarm bell rang out, and "men killed each other in a sort of senseless spite." Fires were lit, the whole town, from governor to riff-raff, ran around mad with excitement, but not knowing what they were excited about. And at the center of the frenzy, were a few men possessed with devils, waiting for an unwilling Messiah, Stavroguin. Each of the conspirators has but one of Stavroguin's cast-off theories, each has but one more plan for depersonalization and slavery. As one of them, Shigalov, puts it, "Starting from unlimited freedom, I arrive at unlimited despotism" (Shigalovism is Nietzschean). The world will be divided, as by the Grand Inquisitor in a later novel, into masters and slaves. "One tenth enjoys absolute liberty and unbounded power over the other nine tenths." No one cares for justice; there is no law but that of the strongest. Smash sanity and order and "Russia will be overwhelmed with darkness; the earth will weep for its old gods." And then the man-god will emerge from hiding.

Kirillov understood the kind of figure who would appear, emerging to defy God, pain, and terror.

There will be a new man, happy and proud, for whom it will be
the same to live or not to live. He will be the new man. He who
will conquer pain and terror will become himself a god. Then
there will be a new life, a new man; everything will be new
. . . then they will divide history into two parts: from the
gorilla to the annihilation of God and from the annihilation of
God to the transformation of the earth. Man will be God and
will be transformed and things will be transformed and thoughts
and all feelings.

The language is a parody of St. Paul and the Book of Revelation
(a Dostoevsky favorite), a parody of Holy Baptism and the Resurrection. A new creature will be born, and with him a new history.
But first one man must die so that the others may live; a sacrifice
must be willingly made. Kirillov accepts the logic of his parody;
Stavroguin and Ivan do not. They try to convince themselves that
it is not necessary to be humble, to die to oneself, not necessary to
die in any way. As Ivan says to himself, "Nothing need be destroyed
. . . we only need to destroy the idea of God in man . . . everything will begin anew. Men will unite to take from life all it can give,
but only for joy and happiness in the present world. Man will be
lifted up with a spirit of divine Titanic pride and the man-god will
appear." But he is by no means sure he wants this to come to pass.
Before he can make up his mind about this and all else, his mind
gives way and, like Nietzsche, he becomes a patient nursed by
women. He had not been able to decide which was right, Titanism
or the Gospel, Truth or Parody.

Dostoevsky himself knew what he wanted; it was reconciliation of
men to one another, "the earth untarnished by the Fall." And so
he allowed characters as hopeless as Stavroguin and Versilov to
dream dreams of paradise. He had once seen Claude Lorraine's
"Acis and Galatea" in the Dresden Gallery; he called it "The Golden
Age." It was a picture of "a corner of the Greek archipelago the
way it was some three thousand years ago. Here was man's earthly
paradise . . . O marvelous dream, lofty illusion! The most improbable of all visions, to which mankind throughout its existence
has given its best energies, for which it has sacrificed everything, for

which it has pined and been tormented, for which its prophets were
crucified and killed." Dostoevsky called this dream "the highest Russian thought," the very thought which he developed in his speech
on Pushkin. This dream would, he believed, become a reality in
"the setting sun of the last day of civilization." But the reality would
not be quite like the dream. Something would have altered, some
twist, some shadow, and in the end it would not be paradise at all
but a terrible solitude.

> I picture to myself that war is at an end and strife has ceased.
> After curses, pelting with mud, and hisses, men are left alone
> according to their desire. The great idea of old has left them,
> the great source of strength that till then had nourished and
> fostered them was vanishing like the majestic sun setting in
> Claude Lorraine's picture. It was somehow the last day of
> humanity, and men suddenly understood that they were left
> quite alone, and at once felt terribly forlorn. The great idea of
> immortality would have vanished, and they would have to fill
> its place, and all the wealth of love lavished of old upon Him
> who was immortal would be turned upon the whole of Nature,
> on the world, on man, on every blade of grass.

As Versilov says, "It is a fantasy and a most improbable one," as
improbable as Ivan Karamazov's "The Geological Cataclysm." First
there is strife, then peace, and in the peace a terrible loneliness, and
then mysteriously and abruptly a new love for all things. The
changes are too swift and without transitions.

He did not know the way yet, but he was convinced he knew the
goal. In "The Story of a Ridiculous Man" he described once again
paradise and the fall that brought about the long course of division,
crime, death, and disbelief, as "they began to struggle for separation,
for isolation, for individuality." Mankind had come to think that
"knowledge is higher than feeling, the consciousness of life is higher
than life." And they killed for their ideas and believed that life has
no meaning unless there is universal suffering. The Ridiculous Man
dreams that he believed this so intensely that he wanted to be crucified for the sake of sufferers. And yet when he awoke from his dream

he remembered all the more warmly the original innocence and harmony. It was a dream of "ecstasy, immeasurable ecstasy." "I have seen the truth; I have seen and I know that people can be beautiful and happy without losing the power of living. I will not and cannot believe that evil is the normal condition of mankind." This is why he is called by Dostoevsky himself a ridiculous man—the pathos of an idea that is not wholly illusion or wholly hope.

There are times and characters in his novels when they seem to be saying, "Force it, force it, it will come if you try hard enough: just will it strongly enough and the barriers will fall." But the barriers seldom fall, and the forcing and trying only reinforce the stubborn self-will and bring paralysis on all the sooner. "In one day, in one hour everything could be arranged at once." But it is not arranged. And the artist's conscience does not allow it either. Each character has his own personality, own self-estimation, own theory of history, own breaking point. Each has his own course to follow, governed by his own hypotheses, and arrives at his own end. Dostoevsky seldom falsified; even Stephen Verhovensky's last hours are as implausible and superficial as the rest of his life. A man is to be judged by the depths from which he has to climb rather than by the ideals which he learns to repeat. The Underground Man's problem is anonymity; his answer is caprice and malice. The Ridiculous Man's answer to the same problem is the ideal of reconciliation, but it comes by way of a dream instead of from the crucible of experience, and it rings sweet and hollow. Dostoevsky knew the seductiveness of utopias as well as he knew the frightfulness of political depersonalization. He did not think either was the last word.

In the person and sayings of Father Zossima (*The Brothers Karamazov*) he made a valiant effort to extend the paradisal convictions which had crumbled in his own hands. On no other part of any of his books had he spent so much time as on this section. But much of it he had said before. "Heaven lies within all of us—here it lies hidden in me now, and if I will, it will be revealed to me tomorrow and for all time." Why then do I not reveal it? Is this not the same utopian illusion which he had advanced before only to abandon before the recollection of the intransigence of sin? The only difference seemed to be that Dostoevsky and Father Zossima both were convinced that the Russians were not like other people. They have preserved the "image of Christ," unlike the rich and noble who prefer the justice based on reason that the bourgeoisie of Europe have been preaching ever since the French Revolution. Salvation will come from the Russian people, especially the peasants, who are meek and believing. He did not say how. He knew he had not finished.

He pressed on. "There is only one means of salvation . . . make yourself responsible for all men's sins . . . as soon as you sincerely make yourself responsible for everything and for all men, you will see that it is really so, and that you are to blame for everyone and for all things." Granting the plausibility of corporate sin and corporate responsibility, the question is still open as to how to make oneself responsible. If it were easy, Stavroguin might have accepted the cross he sought, likewise Dmitri, Ivan, Versilov. That is the trouble; it is not easy, for the self is locked, jammed tight behind its door.

He tried again. There is a divine mystery in things. The face of that mystery is "the precious image of Christ." "Much on earth is hidden from us, but to make up for that we have been given a precious mystic sense of our living bond with the other world." The effort is desperate; the brambles thicken, progress is almost stopped. Where is this mystic sense in the Underground Man, or Stavroguin, or Raskolnikov? Even those like Ivan and Kirillov who love the image of Christ cannot make up for his death by moral euphoria. Man without God is a man paralyzed; he is sick and needs a physician. In the story of Raskolnikov and Sonia, then again in the less serious story of Alyosha and the boys, he suggested a way that respected the essential terms of the problem of man without God, and at the same time held out hope.

In short, the way is the way of purgation and compassion. Self-isolated man cannot break out; he can only be rescued. And he cannot be rescued unless his own will is prepared first for purgation.*

* Cf. my essay on the similarity of tragic experience and the dark night of the soul, "The Dark Night of Sisyphus," in *The Climate of Faith in Modern Literature*, ed. Nathan Scott (Seabury, N.Y., 1964).

He must have within him, as Raskolnikov, a wellspring of pity that can respond to the compassion offered him. The conflict inside him between pride and pity can destroy him without this sacrificial offering. With it he can come slowly but surely to life again as a new person. Whether explicitly understood or not, such compassion is Christ-like; Sonia understood the pattern and gloried in it. In her the image of Christ is so real, so living, that it makes transformation of Raskolnikov possible. As Dostoevsky explains, this is "gradual renewal . . . gradual resurrection." Here is no abrupt, unrealistic, transitionless rebirth. It might actually happen. But first there must be a Sonia (Sophia—divine wisdom). A Liza will not do. And so Stavroguin hangs.

Dostoevsky seems to have been tempted again and again to say, "It is easy, just see the truth, and the rest will come." What he does say is: "We are each responsible for all to all, it's only that men don't know it. If they knew it, the world would be paradise at once." Take him at his word; Dostoevsky knew it, and yet the world never became paradise at once for him. The young Alyosha does not find paradise either, but he learns through Father Zossima's compassion for him to tame a group of wild little boys in his own town. He accepted responsibility where the boys' parents had failed, and he taught them to love one another. The story may be too sentimental; that is dictated by the immaturity and innocence of both Alyosha and the boys. It is a parable based on the spiritual dynamics already outlined with strict and scrupulous regard for plausibility in Raskolnikov's case. There is only one thing that is different, and it may be important.

When the boys ask whether they will ever see their dead friend Ilusha again, Alyosha assures them firmly: "Certainly we shall all rise again, certainly we shall see each other and shall tell each other with joy and gladness all that has happened." This conviction, this hope is founded solidly on the experience and memory of compassionate living, not vice versa. It is not utopian, not a dream, in the sense that it springs from wishing alone. Already Alyosha has entered with the boys into a fellowship that is selfless, candid, and glad. And Dostoevsky implies that Alyosha has this charismatic power because he remembered the tears of compassion of his victimized mother and the compassionate wisdom of his foster father Zossima. With "some good, sacred memory preserved from childhood," a man may be saved. "If a man carries many such memories with him into life, he is safe unto the end of his days, and if one has only one good memory left in one's heart, even that may sometime be the means of saving us." The rest of the Karamazovs are destroyed by a willfulness trapped in a circle of its own devising. And like almost all the fictional figures of Dostoevsky's mind, like Nietzsche, and like the Kierkegaardian souls sick unto death with despair, they win their refuge and their prison in the seventh and ultimate solitude.

CHAPTER 7

Journey from Paradise

"Nostalgia is the mark of the human."—Camus

AT THE END OF the nineteenth century Dostoevsky said that "unrest, confusion, and unhappiness is the present lot of man." We do not have to be historians to know that the lawlessness and chaos which he saw approaching, the nihilism and decadence which Nietzsche sensed, were probably not visible to their contemporaries. Dostoevsky and Nietzsche were prophets of a proximate doom. Their apocalyptic sense is now our reading of their, and our, history. We can see that "the Victorian look of confidence, of being at home in the world, of knowing the way around" (Graham Greene) is even more exceptional than ever. The new barbarians have arisen, in Russia, in China, in Germany, and if they have not brought new visions of human dignity they have surely practiced a Titanic will to power on the innocent, the unsuspecting, and the mean.

A century ago isolation and self-isolation were categories for the lives of artists and philosophers. Homelessness, especially metaphysical homelessness, was definitely a marginal situation so far as the masses of people, even educated people, were concerned. At the present time it takes an ostrich to call homelessness marginal. All the continents have been sickened by bouts of mass homelessness, with millions of people driven from their homes by war, revolution, and persecution. Even when citizens have not had to flee, or have not been allowed to flee, they have been systematically subjected to indoctrination that has been designed to remove all traces of ideals that could conflict with the limited needs of the state. Just as Dostoevsky predicted, man has delivered his freedom to the state, at times even willingly. When he has not, he has been crushed or exiled.

Individual rebellion is now almost impossible; only planned social rebellion is permitted in most countries. The time has come when it is possible to look back with nostalgia to a time when an individual could rebel in his own way and for his own reasons. Indeed, it is strange to read Dostoevsky's conviction that rebellion is not a way of life, and remember that it is the way of life of mass-man today, but hardly possible any longer for the individuals of whom he was speaking. And yet there is another side to the life of the masses which we would do well to remember. The masses do not want bread alone ("miracle, mystery, and authority") as Dostoevsky thought; they want the same basic opportunities for a decent life that a minority, an elite, has always had. As individuals they want justice, as peoples they want self-determination, and therefore have had to protest and struggle against imposed arrangements designed to protect someone else's status quo.

The success of the middle-class revolution of the last century was accompanied by a spiritual and ideological complacency that Kierkegaard, Dostoevsky, and Nietsche noted with platitudinous persistence. The achievements of revolutionary goals of the dispossessed and discriminated in our mid-century are likewise accompanied by the unfriendly gibes of those who are in no need of the new benefits. It is sometimes difficult for those in easy circumstances to remember the burdens of those in a state of violence, despair, and indignation. Nevertheless, the cry for justice is in the air, and will probably challenge our conscience for another generation or so.

Within such a context we must read that strange resolve of a character in a play by Gabriel Marcel, appropriately named Pascal: "I accept absolute insecurity." The dispossessed and discriminated everywhere now reject absolute insecurity, and it would be worse than unkind to ask them not to. The middle-class rejected absolute insecurity long ago. Kierkegaard, Nietzsche, and most of Dostoevsky's characters, on the other hand, did accept absolute insecurity, and they knew well what it meant to dwell in the seventh solitude. But for them "absolute" did not mean economic or political insecurity; absolute insecurity was metaphysical only. Kierkegaard, Dostoevsky, and Nietzsche may have been right, along with Marx, in supposing that whoever is preoccupied with material considerations will not be very concerned with God. Is it not probable also that whoever is not obliged to spend his time thinking about jobs and money will have more time to think about God? Of course, there is no guarantee that he will; the rich are not noticeably more spiritual or speculative than the poor. The point is, recent history has parcelled out religious and metaphysical speculation rather unevenly, the largest share going to those who know no economic insecurity, and the smallest to those whose energies and no doubt speculative talents are devoted mainly to actual revolution.

As the outsider of the nineteenth century has been followed by a more faceless mass man seeking his rights to be an individual with a face and name, so the death of God has so far been succeeded by the violent deaths of many men. And with mass killing and brutalization the dignity of man as a whole has been diminished, the ideals of human worth and freedom made shadowy. Once again the Underground Man's plaint is heard: "Whenever we are left to our own devices, and deprived of our bookish rules, we at once grow confused, and lose our way . . . we grow weary of being human beings at all . . . we are ashamed of being human . . . rather we aim at becoming personalities of a general, a fictitious type." Where are now the free spirits, the happy few, the new men, the pioneers? For as many as have travelled the road to eternity through the straits of anxiety and inwardness, the genuine religious converts of our age, so many more have jammed the lock of introversion and despair. The self-conscious, the gratuitous caprice of Dostoevsky's double has given birth to the sickly facsimiles of compulsive desperation. They are legion. The murder of God is a luxury phrase when the murder of man is the order of the day.

Nietzsche never had to face "the silence of God" in a Nazi concentration camp, nor did he ever seem to be aware of the real tragedies in other people's lives. Pampered by self-adulation and familial protectiveness, he skimmed the waters of meanness and cruelty and persecution. To us there is something incredibly irresponsible about his indifference—or was it bourgeois unawareness—and that of Kierkegaard as well. The more serious, indeed the more speculatively inquiring we are now, the less easy is it to evade the need for justice and charity, the less tempting to lock ourselves up in ourselves and sing songs of self-praise. The passion for justice and unity (Camus called it a "nostalgia") need not apologize to Nietzsche or Kierkegaard; rather are they rebuked for their onesidedness. And yet, to do them justice too, we ought to remember that they were the first to demand clarity, unity, honesty, and that our concern owes much to them and their sacrifices. Perhaps in the mind of Camus justice and unity were intimately connected, but he may also have been reflecting the evident need of his and our time for both. Like Kafka he exhorted himself to keep his intellect calm and clear to the end. That is not always possible. And one reason why it is not is that the enemies of justice press hard on the leisure we need to take our time. But more inhibiting still is the yawning metaphysical (spiritual) vacuum bequeathed our century by the nineteenth, and to which Kierkegaard, Dostoevsky, and Nietzsche devoted, and indeed sacrificed, their lives. It is unfair to protest too much that they were not interested in equal opportunities for all or in political or ecclesiastical ecumenicity, when we know they were wrestling in the dark with the powers of homelessness. They, at least, did not live a conceptually hand-to-mouth existence. They accepted very little at face value, and so handed on to later generations tested habits of metaphysical discrimination.

In the spiritual world of Kierkegaard, Dostoevsky, and Nietzsche no account was taken—had yet to be taken—of a pose common to the past two generations, and expressed by Hemingway's "Nobody ever learns anything . . . . We never learn. . . . I did not care what it was all about." This debased currency of the original imprint of the death of God would not need to be mentioned save that it is itself an expression of a present emotional numbness. If, as we are told, depression is now more often met in clinical practice than hysteria, we may suspect that the mind goes numb when the search for identity is continually blocked by a world without inherent categories or values. Bold is the Nietzschean resolve to make rather than find values, desperate the mind that accepts the impossibility of discovering and yet cannot invent. Before numbness reaches rigidity, much scrambling around, trying out distractions, filling up time, cover the middle ground of everyday. In such a psychological climate almost any kind of restlessness gives reason for hope.

Mankind has come a long way since it was normal to think that "the world is charged with the grandeur of God" (Hopkins). Without intending to imply that it was a better time or a better state of mind, I would suggest that at least it was entirely different from the skepticisms of today. Heidegger has not necessarily said the last word when he mournfully counsels waiting until God makes up his mind to return. That assumes that we are fixed and God is not, that God is responsible for his absence and we are not. I should prefer to see Heidegger—and many others—resume the speculation about Being. It is more to the point to say right now that God's grandeur will not be restored to our sight or feeling until God's questionableness is constantly felt, morning, high noon, and night. When God died—if He did—speculation about God seemed to have died too. And that is what must be reborn.

Two generations ago Scott Fitzgerald, in recording his own "waning vitality . . . emotional exhaustion . . . lesion of enthusiasm . . . crack-up," anticipated a condition now almost endemic. With no spiritual center to hold on to, nervous collapse is a permanent threat, and the centers we substitute, through status and party, are of such flimsiness that they crinkle with the slightest breathing of suspicion. We wait out our chronic tiredness for calm after anxiety, for a paradisal *securitas vitae* to take the place of the *insecuritas* we know so well. In the meantime we are not only tired, but extraordinarily touchy. "What a strange and sad thing life is," said Teilhard de Chardin. "We have to face the fact that nothing we are able to touch is the real consistency we are searching for, while what does seem to be the real consistency we are unable to touch." We have dreamed what we have not yet experienced, and the nature of our dream—call it nostalgia—is that it is an inherited symbol of our destiny. If the only paradise we have known is the one we have lost—and everyone has had his little paradises—this does not mean that paradise is not still before us. The transit-sickness from which we suffer could be hunger pangs for God.

Discouragement explains cynicism, but it does not refute dreams. Neither does one nostalgia exclude others. Misled by contemporaries like Camus, we may come to accept the reach of his private nostalgia for justice and unity. But memories of the past and of our own hearts can still disclose a nostalgia even more radical. I would call this the nostalgia for being, the double nostalgia for earth and for heaven, for creation and for the creator. In the same person there can be a love of God—and He is just—so strong that even the counter love of man and earth cannot efface it. Attracted and then repelled by the *incendium amoris* of a Richard Rolle or a Teresa of Avila, we may feel like burying our souls and bodies in warm sand. What seemed real and present to them seems unaccountably bleak to us, and we draw back in dread of suffocation. And yet creation does not satisfy either, and only offers the disconsolate resting-place of the seventh and last solitude. There are moments—to use a Dostoevskian phrase—there are moments when, in prayer or in painting or in music or perhaps in the Cycladean sun, anxiety falls away, and we feel at home. Then we can believe once more in *la recherche du sentier perdu* (Alain-Fournier); the dream has been replaced by a foretaste, and the mind is encouraged to wonder whether we are not made after all for a reality that is by no means dead. The wonder may not legitimately be interpreted as justification for thinking that we could not even feel homeless unless there was a home; wonder and speculation do not have the same weight as the conclusion of a syllogism. But there can be comfort, justice, unity, and peace in this world, even with these men, these minds, and their inherited solitudes. The door is always open, and it is a cruel piece of self-delusion to imagine it already shut. The answer to Ingmar Bergman's question. "Why can't I kill God within me?" is because He is God and we are in His image.

Appendix

WE HAVE A DOUBLE responsibility: to explore the consequences of a radical nihilism, and to try to recover the nostalgia for unity, justice, and earth. On the whole, more artistic and philosophical effort has been spent on the first, and too little on the second. For this reason I have thought it could be useful to recall two perennial alternatives within the country of nostalgia: the passion for God and the passion for the creation. This is why I am appending an essay on St. Augustine and Proust.

In a sense, these alternatives lie outside the central concern of this book—metaphysical homelessness—but only as a memory of home makes the loss of home more poignant and thus suggests a theoretical alternative to what begins to look more and more like psychological paralysis and philosophical dead end. It is more than conceivable that those who are now cornered in extreme positions in which they feel their pride at stake, may treat their dead ends almost as vested interests, and finally even come to believe that there are no alternatives. But there are alternatives, and always have been, and it is a good time to review them.

Remembering Eternity*

RECOGNITION AND RETURN

WHOEVER ONCE REMARKED THAT Proust would have been really profound had he been blessed with the theological insight of St. Augustine, spoke more aptly than he realized. Proust and St. Augustine, if read side by side, call to mind unexpected questions and resemblances. And yet how different they were. The fifth-century Church Father, one of the two greatest theologians of the Christian Church, a strong bishop, a mighty controversialist, imaginative, ardent; Proust, frequenter of Parisian salons and also recluse, an observer of social customs and the human heart, an agnostic. It is doubtful whether they would have liked each other. Even the fact that they both loved their mothers or wrote on memory, love, and time, or that they are known to most readers principally through autobiographical mediums—none of these is quite enough to dispel the sense that they are quite different. It is only when one tries to understand what Proust means by recapturing reality, what Augustine means by recollecting himself, that one speculates as to whether at some level of interpretation the recognition so central to them both is the same return. If it is true to say of Proust that for him there is no cognition, only recognition, it is equally true to say this of St. Augustine. If it is fair to say of Proust's reality that it is himself, it is fair to say of St. Augustine's reality that it is also that which is most real, God. Should one be tempted to say too quickly that Augustine's reality is theological and Proust's sensuous, the argument would stop, at least until it is reopened by suggesting that

* This essay first appeared in *Thought*, XXXIV (Winter, 1959-60). Copyright 1959 by Fordham University, New York, New York.

the theological is usually embodied, in other words, is to be found in the sensuous.

No one has written more movingly of love than these two, not Stendhal or St. Bernard. And yet it is not in their appreciation of passion or the sensuous that they can be most usefully compared. Rather one should notice their different understanding of what is apparently real. For Augustine the surface of life is defined by disquietude, and whatever the depths, they can be reached only if one begins with a clear view of the function of disquietude. For Proust, on the other hand, the surface of life lies open to the intelligence, but unsatisfying because the self lives in separation from its own life, from the present and the past as well as from the future. We could say of both that the surface of life is essentially disintegrated; we should say that its disintegration is a disembodiment. Augustine's restlessness was understood by him many years after he knew he was restless; along the way, the disquietude was like form without matter, spirit without body. Proust's alienation from present and past, from the self he was living and had been, was a tortured ghost looking for the frame and sensibility that make life real. While Augustine's intellect was seeking faith, Proust's time was seeking eternity. The home to which Augustine returns looks like the eternity from which he has never parted. And the real life recaptured by Proust turns out to be an image of eternity. Proust's eternity is not Christ, but it may be an image of Christ.

Any comparison of two such different men raises a serious question of the motive behind the comparison. One can only say that such a juxtaposition is also part of an interior dialogue within the person doing the comparing. One can also say that Proust and Augustine can be appreciated more adequately if viewed side by side. This may be too strong a claim, one that can be justified only by a clearer, longer discussion of the condition of modern man. Less pretentiously, we could justify the claim by suggesting that a sense of unreality has two definably different yet related aspects. The man for whom life is unreal may have come to the point of no return, despair. Most people do not come to that. And even if they do, they spend a large part of their lives in that vast territory known to everyone, boredom.

In current existentialist and psychiatric parlance this state of being is sometimes explained as a sense of emptiness or meaninglessness. If this were all one could mean by boredom or sense of reality, then it would be incorrect to speak of the weariness of Proust or Augustine. If to be bored or weary means to know that one does not know what it is all about, where one is going, what one should be doing, why everything and more especially some things happen the way they do, then it makes little sense to speak of Proust's dissatisfaction or Augustine's disquietude. That they were both separated in some way from what was most real remains, nevertheless, the starting point they have in common. But that they were experiencing the existential anxiety of meaninglessness or of emptiness is just not true at all. Proust knew the difference between real life and unreal life; Augustine knew the difference between restlessness and rest. They knew and they sought; they knew what they were looking for, even if they did not know the way. In the end they discovered that only when one knows the way does he know what he is looking for, and that what he thought he was looking for was only the sense of the experience, not the experience. It is not rest that one seeks but Christ—Augustine found that out. It was not his own past that Proust wanted again, but a real present. And yet they were not far wrong compared to those of us who, depressed and without vision, wait rather than seek, born sightless and therefore almost without hope.

The difference between Proust and Augustine on the one hand and the sightless depressed on the other depends almost exclusively on the content of memory. The former had something to remember; the latter do not seem to. One recalls the conviction of Father Zossima in *The Brothers Karamazov* of the importance of memories of one's childhood. "The vast structure of recollection," as Proust names it, is not so vast that it can be filled outside experience. Not for Proust or Augustine the Platonist belief that everything is to be found in the memory, filled in this life or another, probably another. "Memory is an abyss from which at odd moments a chance resemblance enables us to draw up, restored to life, dead impressions." It is "a rich mineral basin where there is a vast area of extremely varied precious desposits." "We find a little of everything in our memory; it is a sort of pharmacy, or chemical laboratory." Well, not quite everything. The memories of some people do not seem to contain the way of salvation that is contained in the memories of others. And when Augustine and Proust relive their memories, they are only too aware that they are reliving what they have already experienced in this life, what in fact was put in not many years before. They do not appeal to any pre-existence of the person or his soul to explain what they find, except in one hauntingly poignant passage where Proust says that "everything is arranged in this life as though we entered it carrying the burden of obligations contracted in a former life." But obligations and moral principles aside—and these are not what Proust was looking for—when life is recaptured, it is the immediate not the discontinued past. As for Augustine, he never supposed that he was returning to a pre-existent knowledge of Christ, but rather to the Christ that his Catholic mother had told him of in childhood.

Of memory itself they were both in awe. It is difficult to keep in mind their favorite coinages of recollection. Was it Proust or Augustine who wrote of "the fields and vast palaces of memory," "the vast recesses, the hidden and unsearchable caverns of memory," "the huge court of my memory," "the same storehouse of memory," "a spreading, limitless room within me," "the innumerable fields and dens and caverns of my memory"? Augustine was as impressed as Proust by the arrangement as well as the capaciousness of this aspect of the soul. It was Proust not Augustine, however, who understood more clearly that memory shares in the fallen state of man, that therefore there are two kinds of memory, voluntary and involuntary, and that they deliver significantly different realities to the conscious mind. Augustine is so much in awe of the vastness of memory, of all it can contain, that he seems for a while to forget why he is analyzing it. Proust never forgets, and his distinction between the two memories is the reason. The one memory, deliberate recollection, cannot restore reality as it once was; the other memory, accidental, affective, does more than restore, it creates reality as it should have been. The seeking, the research into the past, turns out to be a creation, not from nothing, but from a matter without form. And if one asks, "What is the matter?", affective memory speaks up, and tells the story that lies beyond all explanations. The answer to the question is a reality and sense of reality.

Whatever is true and real lives outside the intellect, inhering in material objects. "The most insignificant gesture, the simplest act remained enclosed as it were in a thousand jars." Even "our arms and legs are full of sleeping memories of the past." Call this what you will, a theory of association—Proust was obsessed by the obduracy of experience, its independence of the intellect, its freedom to come and go despite any effort of the will. The reality of the association is attested to by the disappearance from the mind of its usual habits of effort and detachment. To remember an event, a place, or a person, even a feeling, it is relatively easy to recall specific features. But one remains a spectator. To remember in such a manner that it is as if the past were present, and as if one were present oneself, with all one's senses responding freely to a certain occasion, that is another story, and a more interesting one. A dog barks away on a warm night in the quiet countryside, the spring peepers fill the night air, the deer nibble the dogwood by the stone wall, such are the signals that call out, recall a society of memories fully equipped with burgeoning sensations. It only takes, Proust told us, one simple event to resurrect a fully felt society of occasions. Each man and woman owns a finite number, a very small number of such signals. It takes only one to resurrect a portion of time so complete that if the natural intelligence were to try to reconstruct it, a disproportionate amount of one's life would be consumed. "The taste of a madeleine dipped in tea, a metallic sound, the feeling of uneven steps," three sensations meaningless in themselves, but associated in the mind with realms of the past, with Combray, Balbec, Venice. Again one is in Combray or Balbec or Venice, just as one was there years before. No, not just like that, for at that time one could not grasp everything, all was slipping away before one could put it in order. And now after such an interval, this intermittent world is transformed into a stable but transfigured world in which we are thoroughly at home.

Certainly the first sensation of renewal is felicity, as absent awhile from anxiety or apprehensiveness the soul rests in its own, its earned entourage and climate. But the felicity, like all sensations of satisfaction, arises solely from the mind's agreement that what it had long looked for is now reborn and present. Time has been embodied in things and events and persons. "It is because they contain the past that human bodies can so much hurt those who love them, because they contain so many memories." Somewhere Proust speaks of human beings as jars that contain the realities of other people; one is less real when someone else dies. "For after death Time leaves the body and memories are obliterated in her who exists no longer and soon will be in him they still torture, memories which perish with the desire of the living body." And so it seems that one spends his life seeing a reality, a true life, that disappears when the material objects that call it forth themselves disappear. Over all Proust's work hovers this cloud of futility, the special futility that goes with mortal achievement. Every parting is a foreshadowing of the final separation of the living from the dead. A human being, time-worn, is unreal compared to the actuality of experience reborn in the affective moment. As the world outside dies, so the possible life within dies too, until we are but a shell. So long as the material signs exist, we, towering over our own past, defined by these signs, live on, albeit experiencing the weariness of the weight of life. Deep within the reality compounded of sign and its associated past lingers the sweet pain that admits fond realization and inevitable separation.

Life is worth, and yet hardly worth, such resurrection. There is something frightening if something vaguely promising and profound in Proust's aside that resurrection of the body might be thought of as a phenomenon of memory. We know too much of the fate of memory's resurrection to put much stock in this particular analogy. And yet it is theologically permissible to think that we are remembered by God as well as by each other. Should that be true, our re-embodiment could be accomplished by association, the nostalgic association of those who are at home in Christ. Is there an unexpected truth in the implication that not only are men resurrected together, but the resurrection of each depends on that of some

others? Picture the saints waiting patiently for those with whom
they passed their lives, to join them, and through association, moral,
sensual, religious, to re-embody them as timeless persons. But timeless though they may become, they were waiting at the end of their
striving in time. Though they wait, their new embodiment arises
from the free association of all the unexpected meetings and decid-
ings, sensibilities and sensations. Whatever religious truth there may
be in this transfiguration of a Proustian aside, it is the pattern of
such transfiguration that should attract our attention in a compara-
tive glance at the reaches of Augustine and Proust. A suggestion, an
implication, an image, a participation in the power of suggestion,
implication, image. Their reaches are covered by a similar formula,
but the similarity to each other should not distract us from the question as to the nature of the pattern both reflect. At the most important moment they speak the same language, a fact more important
than the apparent divergence in the contents of their recognition.
The language, not the content, marks them as bearers of a word not
their own, embodied, enfleshed in their common, human pattern of
recognition and return.

AUGUSTINE: THE SEEKER AFTER GOD

At the time when Augustine was beginning to teach in Tagaste, a
friend he had known from childhood took sick, was baptized, recovered briefly, and then died. In the short period of recovery Augustine mocked his friend for having been baptized. When he died,
Augustine's "heart was black with grief." He "became a great
enigma (*quaestio*) to himself." He could not understand why his
soul was so sad, so disquieted. "Why art thou so full of heaviness,
O my soul? and why art thou so disquieted within me?" (Ps. 42).
And he could not reply with the Psalmist, "O put thy trust in God."
He hated all things, "hated the very light itself, and all that was not
painful and wearisome, save only tears." He marveled that his friend
should be dead and he still alive, and like Proust he "feared to die
lest thereby he should die wholly whom I had loved so deeply." It

would seem as if Proust and Augustine shared the same starting point, the conviction that reality depends on memory, or rather memory on reality. Yet why should a man be an enigma to himself if he did not half believe that reality is not meant to depend on memory? Why cannot all men take the death of their friends for granted? While Proust came to terms with grief at the death of Albertine as soon as he became curious about his grief, Augustine calmed down only by taking in new "seeds from which new griefs should spring." "That first grief had pierced so easily and so deeply only because I had spilt out my soul upon the sand, in loving a mortal man as if he were never to die." He had not learned his lesson, the lesson—Proust's—that friendship is a delusion. Nor could he have said, like Proust, "Never should I find again that divine thing, a person with whom I might talk freely of everything, in whom I might confide." On the contrary he spoke of "my inability to be happy without friends, for truly I loved my friends for their own sake, and I knew that I was in turn so loved by them." Grief did not cause Proust to become a question to himself, neither grief nor any other experience. This is the hallmark of Augustinian self-knowledge.

"Man is a great deep," "I cannot totally grasp what I am," says Augustine. "What then am I, O my God? What nature am I?" Man is a mystery to himself, for he contains within himself intimations of infinity. He is made for something that is better than he knows, and this he can feel. "There is something of man that the very spirit of man that is in him does not know." How else can one account for the extraordinary and equally mysterious disquietude which is such a permanent feature of all but the most insensitive temperaments? Some men, like Augustine, are to be defined almost exclusively by their disquietude. It is not by chance that the following line is the most famous of all Augustine's sayings, "Our hearts are restless until they rest in Thee." As a saying it speaks to other hearts, and to readers of the *Confessions*, it is the signature of a personality. In it are condition and explanation and hope. He could not have said it after the death of his friend. Proust could never have said it. It is the classic religious statement of the human condition. Today it is almost a truism, at least in so far as one ignores the explanation and hears only the expression of universal anxiety. Nor does a man have to believe in God to think that disquietude cannot be comforted by fortune or therapy. Proust himself, at the end of his quest, admits to a feeling of profound fatigue, that poor relation of disquietude.

Disquietude is only a symptom and an effect of a state of being which needs to be more fully defined, the state of dispersion and fragmentation. To feel oneself split, torn apart, scattered, is to reflect a lack of spiritual unity, direction, meaning. It is the characteristic state of most modern minds. This is what makes Augustine seem contemporary to the twentieth century: "I collect myself out of that broken state in which my very being was torn asunder because I was turned away from thee, the One, and wasted myself upon the many." For him to collect himself meant to recollect himself. He had the good fortune to have a self to recollect that had been wasted in youth. Not everyone can return to himself in the way Augustine did. We are ruled, to parody Proust, by that inexorable law that says there will be no resurrection except in association with others. We are not raised alone; we do not return alone. The return of recollection itself depends on what others have allowed us to know and to hope for. Therefore, the greatest tragedy occurs when for the sake of association, friendship, a person freely binds himself to those who are less free than himself, and who do not own the vision of salvation. Augustine never suffered from this hopeless barrenness. When he says, "I became to myself a barren land," he is aware, as always, of two possible states of being, fullness and emptiness, communion and dispersion. Not for him the faint malaise of suspicion that all is not as it should be. Such a state may send a man to a psychiatrist but not turn him into the seeker and questioner that Augustine became. "I, arrogant and depressed, weary and restless, wandered further and further from you." His wandering was not spoiled by arrogance or depression, his wandering was a pilgrimage.

And yet it would be oversimple in the extreme if one tried to give the impression that Augustine like so many of our time was only looking for rest, peace of mind or soul. "Rest in Him and you shall be at peace." "Who shall grant me rest in Thee?" Two men may seek rest, but what they seek will differ vastly because they suffer from such different ills. There are weary men who never seem to have worked or adventured enough to be tired, and there are desperately energetic men, like Augustine, whose vision and purpose are being continually thwarted by inner conflict. "Mad on my way to sanity, dying on my way to life," he "still shrank from dying unto death and living unto life." He could look upon other things and see that they owed their being to God. He was ravished by God's beauty, yet soon torn away from Him by his own weight, "Carnal habit was that weight." "What still held me tight bound was my need of a woman." Like Plato or Plotinus, by force and energy of his disciplined intellect, he ascended through the stages of contemplation until he saw "Your invisible things which are understood by the things that are made." His "trembling glance" had "arrived at That Which Is." But he found that he was in chains, or to coin a more accurate figure, at the end of an elastic leash which pulled him back to a self still in strife. "My two wills, one old, one new, one carnal, one spiritual, were in conflict and in their conflict wasted my soul." "Why this monstrousness?" Why this "sickness of the soul?" The mystery of inner conflict of the will is dark. Symbolic explanations of original sin are so much less important than the universality of the conflict itself. For the conflict, dispersion and fragmentation, is not only the effect of a mysterious fateful past act but also the inner symbol of the mystery of Christ's own brokenness in His atoning sacrifice. We are broken in Him, and He reunifies us by the redeeming Cross and Passion. To absorb this truth is to turn and collect oneself from one's wandering.

So it happened to Augustine. The writings of the Platonists had showed nothing of the face of the love of Jesus Christ, "the tears of confession, Your sacrifice, and afflicted spirit, a contrite and humbled heart, the salvation of Your people, the espoused city, the promise of the Holy Spirit, the chalice of our redemption." He was "not yet lowly enough to hold the lowly Jesus as my God." A disobedient will coupled with an intellect seeking faith and yet not satisfied with an intellectual answer, that is the peculiar spiritual mixture that spells out Augustinian disquietude. Twist and turn though he might, he could not break the grip that inhibited freedom, until he could recognize the Way, the very pattern of his condition. "This is my body which is broken for you." We are the body of Christ, broken for each other. Until this pattern is recognized for what it is, a theological symbol, man must pray with Augustine, "Set us free who now beseech Thee, and not only us, but those also who have never besought Thee—that they may turn to Thee and be made free." We must seek for those who do not seek, for those perhaps who cannot seek until we pray for them. Such is the implication of Augustine's intercession. Interior frustration resembles slavery inasmuch as the intellect and the will cannot attach themselves permanently to their end. Slavery must be transformed from slavery to oneself to slavery for all. "Whoever would be great among you must be your servant, and whoever would be first among you must be slave of all."

There is a blind restlessness that tosses souls back and forth without betraying its cause, because it has no goal, no final cause. Some seek distraction, diversion as Pascal put it, in order to avoid facing serious questions; others do not seek at all, but, taking for granted the conventional order, move about within it, and betray their lack of freedom in the unsettled manner of their acceptance of what they will not give up. Squirrels in the cage, men and women boxed in a conventionality that protects and insults them, they take for granted that the only freedom they can bear is restlessness itself. Not for them the burning of the young man who came to Carthage. He was not yet in love but was in love with love. With a secret need of love he loved even before he found anyone to love. And so he sought for someone to love, hating security, the security without love, and famished for want of the interior food that is God. His "one delight was to love and be loved," his one delight and his longing. To Carthage, then, he came, "where a cauldron of shameful loves clamored noisily from every side." He longed to love and be loved, "but most when I obtained the enjoyment of the body of the person who loved me." Someone else has said that to be a person is to be in search of a person. This applies above all to Augustine's longing.

"We go not by walking but by loving," and we do not find out where we are going until we love. That great man's quest was an exercise in longing, and like anyone else he was at first incapable of discriminating between one person and another as the object of his longing. He could not say, "I long for Thee with unquenchable longing." All he knew, from his secret need, was that "longing (*desiderium*) is the heart's treasure." Later he was able to pray, "order in me love," but only after a long and nearly disastrous experience of disorder.

We have said that Augustine's disquietude is to be distinguished from that of Proust by his sense of the human enigma or mystery. To leave it at that would be to omit the dynamic nature of the enigma, the strange and fateful attraction that is secretly exerted by the questionability of the self, that the soul responds to with longing. Augustine has said, "Give me a lover and he will know what I am talking about." How many men and women know the kind of lover Augustine had in mind—a lover who smashes and breaks until he has reached his love, or until he is himself destroyed? Longing is like an obsession, grim, single-minded, compulsive, fated to consume itself and all intermediary objects until it is transformed by union with its love or destroyed. The very word "longing" tells of a distance between the soul and its end, the person one essentially seeks. To long is to stretch every nerve, to be bound and racked so that every nerve is stretched. To long is to become aware of the self as an abyss, yawning for fulfillment. The lovesick heart is no different from the homesick heart. Both are nostalgic expressions of a soul that feels it is meant to possess and be possessed, joined as one with some other. The longing heart, the lonely heart, does not seek rest as such; it seeks "rest in Thee." And this is the binding up in union of the broken parts of the social body, the body of Christ. Every time two are joined together, Christ's body is joined together. This is the pattern and the reality of religious life. The whole life of the good Christian is a holy longing; that is our life, to be exercised by "longing." "What is the worship of God but the love of Him, whereby now we long to see Him?" The answer is that love and longing are not quite the same, and that worship is more than longing. He who worships does not merely long for union with God, his longing is answered by God, the distance between them bridged by Christ. In the measure of His sacrifice, of His body broken for man, man's distance and dispersion are forgotten in communion with God. "It is in your gift that we rest," the gift of God's love shown in His sacrifice for mankind. Augustine speaks a profoundly moving truth when he adds, "My love is my weight, wherever I go my love is what brings me there." We have heard him confess the weight of carnal habit, a habit which grew when love was misdirected in his youth. Wherever he goes, up or down, shamefully or gloriously, love is the gravitational principle, the energy and the direction, the plea for union and recollection.

Of course, one must distinguish between a holy and unholy longing, between the longing for God and the sensual longing for another person. But Augustine is not being heretical when he boldly advises us to look for a real lover if we are to understand him. In some curious way Augustine himself in spite of his sexual wanderings, and in spite of a fidelity to one mistress for a number of years, was not aware of having experienced communion in sexual love. He understood communion between friends, and that between son and mother. But between him and his mistress there "was principally the sheer habit of sating a lust that could never be satisfied." So Augustine tells us in justification for throwing her off so that he could marry a young girl, presumably of better family, to please his mother. We are, therefore, surprised to read, "My heart which had held her very dear was broken and wounded and shed blood." Perhaps he knew more of communion with his mistress than he would admit. Other readers have found his parting with his mistress, mother of his beloved son Adeodatus, shockingly callous. That may be, and yet we may guess that his passionate longing for God may have been schooled in his love for the woman without name whom he sent back to Africa when he was twenty-nine years old. "Come, Lord, work upon us, call us back, set us on fire and clasp us close, be fragrant to us, draw us to Thy loveliness; let us love, let us run to Thee." "I long for Thee, O Justice and Innocence, Joy and Beauty of the clear of sight, I long for Thee with unquenchable longing."

We can only repeat to ourselves his own requirement: give me a lover and he will understand.

As Graham Greene has suggested, "The words of human love have been used by the saints to describe their vision of God, and so, I suppose, we might use the terms of prayer, meditation, contemplation to explain the intensity of love we feel for a woman." The old Prayer Book clause from the marriage service, "with my body I thee worship" has proved too embarrassing for the puritanical to continue using, and yet outside the marriage service the same people say, "I adore you." Who can tell whether the word "adoration" belongs primarily to secular or to religious love? The non-Catholic Christian, not to say the non-Christian, is made uncomfortable by the freedom with which the saints use the imagery of human love to describe their journey toward and communion with God. But this discomfort is part of a regrettable separation in modern man's thinking about spirit and flesh. The same person who finds it natural to speak openly and explicitly about sex will feel there is something improper about speaking of God, in whom he does not believe, in amorous metaphors. Human love has sunk for many persons to the level of flesh starved for spirit. But even when this is not so, and the discomfort persists when the language of religion and human love are interchanged, it is remarkable how little such persons experience a love of God which requires the terminology of the most intense personal encounter. Of the two tests of true religion, charity and adoration, the first may seem to persist in isolation when the habit of the second has been broken. It is doubtful whether charity can survive for long after the total disappearance of adoring worship. Love of God and love of neighbor are intertwined; if to love one's neighbor means that one loves him in God, to love God is to feel impelled to become godlike and love one's neighbor. The time can come in a person's life —or a civilization's—when charity persists as a convention which is justified only in terms of self-interest, and that is usually a time when the very phrase, "the love of God," has become meaningless, and his adoration an abandoned cult, the remnants of which are regarded by the sophisticated as superstition.

Contemporary readers of Augustine's *Confessions* are usually
made uneasy by several things; by his preference for a celibate life,
the constant praying, and the ardent rhetoric. Toward the last the
reader may have mixed feelings, or inhibited reluctance to admit
that it is proper to speak with ardor, and a secret admiration for the
Olympian strength of his passion. One has only to consider briefly
the normal response to the several parts of the following sentence,
typical of the *Confessions,* to realize how distant this man is from the
mid-twentieth century. "I longed after immortal wisdom, I had
begun that journey upwards by which I was to return to You . . .
How did I then burn." Today one reads with uneasiness even
Socrates' exhortation to pursue truth, and we would feel slightly
ridiculous if our teachers expected us to talk this way in the street.
The very word "truth" seems to have lost its right to be capitalized.
We do not believe in absolutes any more. Nor can we couple wisdom
and immortality without the same discomposure. In a sense, there
is something right about the unwillingness or inability to conceive of
truth apart from reality, to conceive of truth as a disembodied
essence. Unfortunately, it is now just as difficult for us to conceive of
anything embodied as permanent either. The metaphors of love,
longing, burning, are similarly displeasing in this context, as we
have pointed out. In some way, the characteristic Augustinian metaphor of journey and return is the most alien of all, for there is a
secret seduction in it which can be felt and which must, therefore,
be resisted. There are many souls today who would be happy if life
could be described fairly as a return to something stable and lovely.
In this lies the peculiar appeal of Augustine, even to those who feel
farthest from his terminus of adoration. One can remain unmoved
by the outbursts of praise that besprinkle his *Confessions,* "beauty
of beauties," "O loveliness that does not deceive, loveliness happy
and abiding" (*dulcedo non fallax, dulcedo felix et secura*). It is
easy to shrug them off; it is not so easy to pass over his metaphor of
life as a return, even to a happiness we think we do not and cannot
know. This is the figure which is the special feature of Augustinian
introspection, the figure which immediately links his mind with that
of Proust.

Like Dostoevsky, the young Augustine was a God-seeker. "And what is this God? I asked the earth and it answered, 'I am not He,' and all things that are in the earth made the same confession. 'We are not your God; seek higher.' " He searched for God in Manicheism and Platonism. "I went out of myself in search for You, and did not find the God of my heart." He did not want a philosopher's God; he wanted what we would now call an existentialist's God, the God of his heart, a God to worship, not just a God to know about. He asked "the whole frame of the universe about God and it answered, 'I am not He, but He made me.' " He is impressed by the contingency of all things, their creatureliness; he wonders at the universal testimony to God's creating hand. And in his search for God he wonders equally at the interior vastness of man. "Here are men going afar to marvel at the heights of mountains . . . yet leaving themselves unnoticed." But although he remembers God as he remembers himself and all he has been taught, all he has seen, done, known, the God of his voluntary memory is likewise not the God of his heart. "He is in the most secret place of the heart, yet the heart has strayed from Him." One cannot exaggerate the difference in Augustine's thinking between the God who is the creator of a contingent world, whose "eternal power and deity," to quote St. Paul, "has been clearly perceived in the things that have been made," and "the God of my heart" from whom men have strayed. It is not only that this is someone to worship; it is someone from whom one has fled. This should seem to contradict the claim that Augustine was a God-seeker; for how can one seek if one is fleeing? At the very moment that a man's mind may be groping with theological and metaphysical questions, his heart may have attached itself to some part of God's creation. At the very moment that a man admires liturgy, he may be desiring possession of that which distracts him from liturgy. As Dostoevsky put it, "I can't endure the thought that a man of lofty mind and heart begins with the ideal of the Madonna and ends with the ideal of Sodom. What's still more awful is that a man with the ideal of Sodom in his soul does not renounce the ideal of the Madonna, and his heart may be on fire with that ideal, genuinely on fire." Far from there being a mere conflict between head and heart, there can be as Augustine as well as Dostoevsky knew, a conflict within the heart itself, or as he thought of it, between two wills. Two kinds of seeking go on at the same time; the heart is more than fully engaged, and fully divided.

This is a view into the human soul that so distresses some men and women that they try to deny the genuineness of the longing for God. They ask, "How can a man pretend to long for God if he takes such pleasure in wandering away from Him?" For the tidy mind this paradox is insoluble, except by a refusal to take it seriously. For Augustine, the truth about man's condition starts out from this paradox. "Let truth," he says, "the light of my heart, speak to me, not my own darkness." Man has within him both darkness and light. "There is but a dim light in men; let them walk, let them walk, lest darkness overtake them." What darkness? "My own darkness," he answers. If truth is the light, then what truth? "They hate truth when it accuses them." To worship God in spirit and in truth means to worship a God whose truth is surely not only larger and stranger than the human heart, but condemnatory of human sensualism and sentimentality. "I fell away and my sight was darkened; but from that depth, even from that depth, I loved Thee. I wandered afar, but I remembered Thee, I heard Thy voice behind me calling me to return, but I could scarcely hear it for the tumult of my unquieted passions." Darkened by the obscurity of misdirection of one's life, stirred into compulsive restlessness by the dispersion of one's desires and affections, even then memory holds the door open and the voice calling for a return can be faintly heard. However far the soul wanders from its resting place, the beginning and the end, the signals leap out into the world and are picked up by the wanderer in the desert. "And now behold I return to Thy fountain, panting and with burning thirst . . . . Let me not be my own life . . . . In Thee I live again." Let us turn to God and be healed. "Let us now return to Thee, O Lord, that we may not be overturned." Or, as the Penitential Office of the Book of Common Prayer says, "Turn thou us, O good Lord, and so shall we be turned."

"Because we do not hope to turn again" (Eliot), we obdurately resist the call contained in those lines. Such a turning would be a crisis too complete. What we normally think of as a crisis is a set of circumstances which forces impossibly difficult decisions or endurance on us. What we object to in a crisis is the unwantedness of it, the avalanche-like aspect of its happening. Only rarely does a person think of a crisis as a welcome opportunity for which he has been longing. This is in part why Augustine's repeated exhortations to turn and return ring a little irrelevantly in our hearing. Nevertheless, the call is heard, however faintly, and more often than is admitted. To be told that wherever we go and whatever we do, we cannot stray in fact, but only in intention, from God, is to tease the mind with the suggestion of a mystery about human nature. What if there should be something in this, we ask ourselves. What if there is something or someone responsive who not only will not let us escape or forget him, but who draws us closer to him? The fact that distinguishes Christians from other religious people is their remembrance of Christ, the Word made flesh. Augustine often refers to this, particularly when he wants to show what Christianity has that Platonism does not have. It has Christ, God become man, who lived and died and rose again for mankind. And then He went away; having entered history as we do, He departed from history as we depart. Augustine's simple comment is, "For He went away, and behold He is still Here." He does not mean only that He left the Holy Spirit, the Comforter. He is still here in the Church and the Sacraments, the new body of Christ, the center of a new history. As St. Leo has said, "That which was visible in our Redeemer has now passed into the Sacraments." Augustine, who never forgot that he had become a "dispenser of His Sacraments," said, "If you are the body of Christ and His members, then that which is on the altar is the mystery of yourselves, receive the mystery of yourselves." The Church is by nature sacramental, mysterious, and in its mystery Christ is found, in the heart of each of its members, and in the whole. And yet it must be admitted that although "Thou dost never depart from us, with difficulty we return to Thee." The return depends on our choosing, our freedom, not on the gift, the grace, the charity, always available. People may take their time about returning because they trust that God in Christ will never depart from them. They use their freedom to explore those things which are actually and emotionally less certain. Since all things participate in God's power, it is impossible to cut oneself off completely; it is only possible to want to cut oneself off.

When Augustine says "that light was within, I looking outward," he is thinking of "the lowly Jesus," not the God of the Platonists, belief in whom did not convert his own splintered will. Belief in God by itself did not give Augustine his sense of return. He had made a journey upward, but he had not yet returned. Although the language looks Platonic, even the language of his conversion, it concerns a moral turning, not an intellectual achievement. "Late have I loved Thee, O beauty, so ancient and so new; late have I loved Thee. For behold Thou wert within me and I outside. Thou wert with me, and I was not with Thee." The play on "with" and "within" in English, or *intus* and *cum* in Latin, suggests the distinction between the metaphysical category of immanence or participation and the moral category of responsibility. This is a God who is the secret of myself and at the same time the self's active companion. And yet it is a God who can be praised as beautiful, a marvel to behold, a perfection and excitement to return to. "Thou wert there before me, but I had gone away from myself, and I could not find myself much less Thee." There is no more arresting sentence in Augustine than this. It contains the characteristic reference to the journey out and the return, and then opens up, as only Augustine could, the question of human self-knowledge, obliquely, as an afterthought. Augustine whose *Confessions* is the first attempt at interior autobiography, had pretended that he was seeking God, not knowledge of self. And in the course of his search, he not only tells much about himself, he discovers that it is only when he returned to God that he came to know himself. This is not a by-product of seeking God so much as that a return to God is a return to self. Whether one seeks God or self, one will find neither in the usual place. "Seek what you seek, but it is not where you seek it." Or as T. S. Eliot has put it, "The way leads towards possession of what you have sought for in the wrong place."

Had Augustine been trying to find himself, had he, for example, been undergoing a course in psychoanalysis, it is doubtful whether he would have been converted. However much a person comes to know himself through psychoanalysis, it often seems that the more he comes to know about himself, the less he becomes capable of knowing God. In this respect Augustinian self-knowledge is radically different. "Let me know myself, Lord, and I shall know Thee." The agnostic who undergoes psychoanalysis can become acquainted with the origins of his emotional difficulties and may at least come to know what he ought to face openly. But if he has never known or felt that holy longing which is the Augustinian disquietude, it is unlikely that psychoanalysis will give it to him. Without this disquietude Augustinian self-knowledge would lack its essential motive, and the motive is the only guarantee of the end. Augustine himself, unlike many mid-twentieth-century agnostics, had been given a Christian upbringing; he always knew that the Church was waiting for him, and that his mother was watching and praying. If psychoanalysis could expose in each patient a universal disquietude, which could be interpreted to be holy longing, then the role of the priest could begin smoothly from where the psychotherapist left off. Too many of those who have been psychoanalyzed assume, however, that they know all there is to know about themselves. It is natural that after the expense of so much money and so many confidences they should want to think this. Augustine would want to say, with Kierkegaard, that until a person has become acquainted with his "God-relationship" such self-knowledge is incomplete. He had asked, "What could be closer to me than myself?" We can reply, in his manner, "nothing but God." But only an inadequate metaphysics would attempt to measure the distance of self from self, and self from God, and then to compare the two. To learn the truth about oneself and not to learn that God is that truth, that man will always be frustrated until he learns to "adore the mystery of love" (Charles Williams), is to become inadequately acquainted with the dynamic of human nature. When Augustine exhorts us to return to our own heart that we may find Him, he is assuming from his own experience that his own heart and the God of that heart are inextricably and mysteriously intertwined.

"O sinners, return to your own heart and abide in Him that made you." "The Word Himself calls to you to return, and with Him is the place of peace that shall not be broken." Not only does religious psychoanalysis reach a different conclusion from medical psychoanalysis, it also begins with a different assumption, the assumption of sinfulness. Ordinary psychotherapy, on the contrary, begins with the assumption that the individual has become so enslaved, so little responsible, that psychotherapy is needed that he may become free. Now one of the chief signs of freedom is the ability of a person to accept his responsibility for real, not imagined, sinfulness. If this is true, how then do we explain Augustine's Pauline dismay when confronted by a conflict within him which he could not by thinking resolve? "Why this monstrousness? And what is the root of it? The mind gives itself an order and is resisted. . . . It is no monstrousness, but a sickness of the soul." Or as St. Paul expressed the same dilemma: "I do not understand my own actions. For I do not do what I want, but I do the very thing I hate . . . So then it is no longer I that do it, but sin that dwells within me." It may be suggested that the dilemma as posed by Paul and Augustine is similar, but not quite the same. Many people would admit shame at being in such a dilemma, but would not admit responsibility or guilt. But Augustine, on the other hand, was able to say: "Being admonished by all this to return to myself, I entered into my own depths, with You as guide, and I was able to do it because You were my helper. I entered, and with the eye of my soul, I saw Your unchangeable light."

What does Augustine mean by "You as guide?" It makes no sense to speak of help until one knows he needs it, until he cannot help himself. Augustine had to be able to say, "Because my will was perverse it changed to lust, and lust yielded to became a habit, and habit not resisted became necessity." As long as he could believe himself capable of controlling himself, he could not understand the real deficiency of Platonism. The attractiveness of Platonism, whether applied to its vision of the good or to a consequent reform of character, arises from a certain confidence that man is capable of all things. Plato and his followers were acquainted with aberration and error, but not with the compulsion to sin. This is why there was no need, as they thought, of a redeemer. In this respect, Old Testament religion does not differ essentially from Platonism, although while the Psalmist would pray for deliverance, the Platonist would depend on his intellect and will. A time comes for many men when neither intellect nor will nor prayer seems to be sufficient. That time came for a whole people in the apocalyptic times preceding Christ's birth; they had the Law, they required a living Way. Many of them, however, like Augustine himself before his conversion were "not yet lowly enough to hold the lowly Jesus as my God." For it is not enough to confess one's incompetence—"the house of my soul is too small to receive Thee. . . . It is all in ruins; do Thou repair it." It is not enough to acknowledge the majesty of the Law or the promises of God. It is not enough, just because for societies as well as for individuals, the will can change to lust, lust to habit, habit to necessity, until too much of their freedom has become determined by the past, by history. The harder one tries to regain one's freedom, it seems, the more tightly one becomes bound. Intense moral effort having failed, because every effort only activates all the demons as well as all the graces, one way alone remains, the Way of Christ. This is the pattern of divine humility. Later in life Augustine prescribed "first humility, second humility, third humility . . . not that there are no other commandments to be named, but unless humility precedes, accompanies, follows," there can be no health, no salvation. Or, as Mr. Eliot has said, "The only wisdom we can hope to acquire is the wisdom of humility: humility is endless." The question is, How do we acquire it?

Christ had said, "I am the Way, the Truth, and the Life." And Augustine himself had had to discover "the way of humility in that the Word was made flesh and dwelt among men." For a long time "the mystery contained in the truth that the Word was made flesh, I could not even faintly glimpse." His pride had to be brought low, by despair at his inability to regulate his concupiscence, and by his lack of strength to enjoy the God even of the Platonists, the God of active contemplation. "Where," he asked, "was that charity which builds us up upon the foundation of humility, which is Christ Jesus?" The writings of the Platonists, so admirable in many ways, the best of the non-Christian world, contained nothing of "that love, the tears of confession, Your sacrifice, an afflicted spirit, a contrite and humbled heart, the salvation of Your people, the espoused city, the promise of the Holy Spirit, the chalice of our redemption." He seized upon the writings of St. Paul, whom he had not been ready for before. He listened with intense interest to the stories of the conversion of well-known Roman officials whom he respected. He longed to be converted himself. But not until he had so despaired of being converted that "a mighty storm arose in me, bringing a mighty rain of tears," was he able to respond to the Apostle's encouragement to "put yet on the Lord Jesus Christ and make not provision for the flesh in its concupiscences." And then "it was as though a light of utter confidence shone in all my heart." "And I heard Thee as one hears in the heart, and there was from that moment no ground of doubt in me."

When he saw the Light, he experienced a moral turning, not merely an intellectual one. And yet this is precisely what Christian truth is. The God that is known in Christ is a moral God whose guidance and help can be received only as it is understood as a Way tried by God himself. This is not a metaphysical truth; it is historical and no less powerful or supreme because it is historical. God's answer is deed, the Word made flesh, God humbling Himself to become man, to live and die as man, and to give Himself completely in all He does, carrying others' burdens. "He who knows the truth (this historical truth) knows that Light (that confidence following conversion), and he that knows the Light knows eternity. Charity knows it. O eternal truth and true love and beloved eternity" *(caritas novit eam; o aeterna veritas, et vera caritas, et cara aeternitas)*. That Truth, that Light, that Eternity—all known as and by Charity, and Charity known as and through Christ, and Christ in the Church, in "the Sacraments of Your Word." A reader of the *Confessions* is impressed by the paeans to Light and Truth. No doubt they are Platonic terms, but in Augustine's mouth they bear a special and warm tone. Light is lovely *(dulce)*; light is interior and eternal, light of my heart *(lumen cordis mei)*. "O Truth, how inwardly did the very marrow of my soul pant for You." This is Christus Veritas, a combination of terms which links history with philosophy, theology with metaphysics. Truth deprived of Christ is morally sterile; Christ as the Way of life is not simply the only truth that one can live by, it is a mystery to be adored and contemplated. There is nothing more mysterious, more intellectually enthralling than the mystery of Christ, the Word made flesh. For it is at one and the same time a paradox of the past, the pattern of the present, the promise of the future. Man cannot comprehend the origin of the paradox, or the power of the pattern, or the glory of the promise. But he can believe in it and live by it. For the religious philosopher, the truth that can be adored is infinitely more profound than the truth that has to be analyzed at arm's length. The philosopher's detachment, his ideal impartiality, may well be an imitation of the contemplative's awe. There is a Truth before which one can only kneel, the Truth that God knelt for mankind, the Truth that men must kneel with and for each other. This truth is in man, has always been in man, but Christ has brought it out into the open once for all. "All the time You were more inward, than the most inward place of my heart." "You stood in the secret places of my soul." "I should be nothing unless You were in me, or rather unless I were in You." This, finally is the structure of the soul, you in me and I in you. Man would be nothing if God were not in him, if God were not sustaining, moving and directing man. Man would also be nothing if he were not in God, partaking of His being and power and pattern.

This is Christian, not Augustinian theology. What distinguishes Augustine's insight into the divine mystery from other theologians' is his special sense that conversion implies recognition. The *Confessions* start out with his wonderment that "no one can call upon Thee without knowing Thee." They culminate in his formula that "We do not say that we have found what was lost unless we know it, how can we know it unless we remember it." Man seeks for happiness in the wrong place. He longs for a proper end to his disquietude, not knowing that all longing can be satisfied only by communion. The mystery of his own being is the mystery of the communion he has been seeking, and in this mystery rests his happiness. But the mystery can be made plain only in the historical pattern of the Word made flesh, and in history the Word is embodied in the Risen Christ. "My faith, Lord, cries to Thee, the faith that Thou hast given me, that Thou hast inbreathed in me through the humanity of Thy Son and by the ministry of Thy Preacher."

The language of theology seems opaque and artificial until the soul descends in torment to the place where no alternative remains except humility. And then the seeking can be transformed into a burning for that peace which the world cannot give, a peace which passeth all understanding. When the soul arrives at this juncture, a new life and a new understanding arise from the embers of the old. The character of the new is an astonishing and heart-warming familiarity. From beginning to end, the Augustinian search is an exercise in the intimacy of man's being, within which the seeker after rest discovers that there is rest in God, then that God is in Christ, then that he has returned to where he began, the built-in image of the cross, disquietude. "In my beginning is my end; in my end is my beginning" (Eliot). The certitude that infallibly accompanies the final discovery that the new is the old—"O Beauty so ancient and so new"—is the certitude of union with God. Man is not alone, he has returned to his home.

PROUST AND THE WORLD OF SELF

In any mind, and most of all in original and developed minds, there are two crucial elements, the basic formula with which it interprets reality, and the peculiar sense of deficiency with which that mind always starts out along its way. Augustine finally was able to envision life as a return and a recognition, but long before he saw this truth, he understood that the surface of the human condition is disquieted. His destiny was to be the discovery that disquietude can be fulfilled only in a return and recognition. Proust, living fourteen hundred years later in a wearier world, no longer waiting in eager "expectation for the revealing of the sons of God" (Paul), also came to see life as some kind of return. But his starting point was quite different. He saw the human state as one of aloneness. "Each of us is indeed alone." But in what way? Everyone is alone in so far as he dies alone. Out of the realization of contingency and finiteness arises the Pascalian astonishment at "being here rather than there; for there is no reason why here rather than there, why now rather than then." Or as Kierkegaard put it, "All existence frightens me, most of all myself." And so, "I stand like a lonely pine tree egoistically shut off, pointing to the skies and casting no shadow, and only the turtle-dove builds its nest in my branches." And why should existence not frighten one, since, as Pascal imagined it, it is as if all men were "in chains, condemned to death, and some were taken off to be killed each day." Mortal men are alone. But for those who can find solace in love, friendship, community of interest, the inescapable solitude can be endured and even for a time forgotten.

Proust has much to say about death, but on the whole it must be said that however much death preoccupies him, he does not ascribe man's essential aloneness to death, but rather to what he holds to be the inevitable unreality of friendship. No man had more affectionate friends than Proust, and yet whenever he writes of friendship it is of friendship as a delusion. No writer speaks more cynically of the human condition, without God and with no friend to take His place. He would expose "the lie which seeks to make us believe that we are not irremediably alone." His novels demonstrate Gabriel Marcel's comment that "we live in a world where betrayal is possible at every moment and in every form: betrayal of all by all and of each by himself." The reason for this is that "the bonds that unite another person to ourselves exist only in our minds" (Proust). Therefore, "we exist alone." Proustian aloneness is the enclosure of mortal man who wishes for a communion which he cannot have. Conscious of and fearful of death, he looks for solace in others, only to find that all betray all, that all are hopelessly boxed up in their own fears and desires. "Man is the creature that cannot emerge from himself, that knows his fellows only in himself; when he asserts the contrary, he is lying."

Proust's hero, Marcel, grieves after Albertine has departed, the girl whom he had kept captive to his desires. Nothing could have been more false than his relationship with her. Her evasiveness is at least pitiable beside his prying and insistence. She could stand no more, ran away, and by accident was killed before he could see her again. He called this the greatest calamity of his life, and yet he admits that he is more curious about the effects of his grief than about the loss of Albertine herself. "It is the tragedy of other people that they are to us merely showcases for the very perishable collections of our own mind." Proustian aloneness does not come mainly either from an anxiety over death or from the bitter experience of betrayal by another, but rather from the inability of the Proustian hero to give himself unreservedly. "We exist only by virtue of what we possess, we possess only what is really present to us, until they are lost to sight." And although he adds, poignantly, "they know of secret paths by which to return to us," we would be rash indeed if we let this promise distract us from the peculiar nature of Proust's understanding of the state of men. Such a being, which can take no satisfaction in loving or being loved, must find some other justification for its existence.

Proust finds justification in memory. If existence were stable, always open to us and at our disposal, then one might find happiness in possession. But the only possessions that can be depended on, that are more or less at our beck and call, that are not closed to us forever, are memories. Of course, this means, as Proust admitted, that whatever justification we find for our existence must acknowledge "the purely mental character of reality." Marcel's grief over Albertine has some resemblance to real grief, until he tries to turn her death into something intellectually interesting to him. We are moved when he says, "Never should I find again that divine thing, a person with whom I might talk freely of everything, in whom I might confide." And he goes on to recall her lips gliding over the surface of his throat and stomach. "All these so pleasant memories" are scarcely examples of "love, which alone is divine." Sensuality, that detachment of the soul from the body, that calculating manipulation of one body by another for the sake of self-satisfaction. "These so pleasant hours," "these so pleasant memories," these remain and are imperishable; truth to tell, these alone are the end of man, for Proust. Has not he confessed: "The world of possibilities has always been more open to me than that of real events . . . reality is never more than an allurement to an unknown element in quest of which we can never progress very far."

To most sensitive persons, it is patronizing to be told that they probably prefer books to people. But Proust would have thought this an unfair description of his attitude toward reality. He would have claimed that it was not so much a question of what he preferred as of what man can have. Man cannot emerge from himself; he must be continually on guard. Proust's is a Kantian world, in which external reality has its character and its charm assigned to it by the viewer. We do not touch others; we only touch ourselves through them. We do not know the intrinsic worth of an experience; we only know that we are trying to get out of it and how it resists us. "We try to discover in things, endeared to us on that account, the spiritual glamor which we ourselves have cast upon them, we are disillusioned, and learn that they are in themselves barren and devoid of the charm which they owed, in our minds, to the association of certain ideas." To try to know someone else is to court disillusionment. The Proustian world is a geography of personal disillusionment. Even places, the last resort of those who fail with persons, even places, are sites of projected needs. "The places that we have known belong now to the little world of space on which we map them for our own convenience." Likewise, the persons that we have known appear to us "only in a succession of momentary flashes. . . . A great weakness, no doubt, for a person to consist merely in a collection of moments; a great strength also; it is dependent upon memory." "Reality will take shape in memory alone." No, it is not great weakness; it is a degrading failure and insult, failure on the part of the person who insults the dignity of other men and women.

Memory holds the key to reality, and though memory is strong, ever capable of bringing back to life the past which we thought was dead, we may judge this estimate of strength as an irony born of despair. In the end, for Proust, reality is reduced to sensation. "An hour is not merely an hour. It is a vase filled with perfumes, sounds, plans, and climates." What we call reality is a certain relationship between these sensations and the memories which surround us at the same time. How real is death itself? Proust's Marcel does not grieve over the loss of a person so much as the loss of his feelings for that person. He does not shudder at the prospect of his own annihilation so much as at the annihilation of his feelings. We do not fear death; we fear that we will no longer feel whatever we feel. This is why the most unsettling experience of all would be the experience of being at someone else's disposal, or of exploring something without the protection of preconceptions or desires. "What an abyss," Proust complains. "What an abyss of uncertainty whenever the mind feels that some part of it has strayed beyond its own borders, when it, the seeker, is at once the dark region through which it must go seeking." Even in the straying beyond itself Proust believes that one brings one's own geography with one. What more desperate account of self-enclosure can be given?

The world of Proust is a sad world. If one lives in it, one takes for granted that neither persons nor places are fixed, except in memory. The fact is, this is what the world is like, not just the Proustian world. What makes Proust's world different is his conviction that this is not all one can say, but that reality is on the one hand more real than what passes and yet is related to that which is past. Proust does not attempt to deny what apparently happens. Persons do die, and disappear. We never see some places again. We never have the same experience twice. We all grow old. There is nothing permanent outside the mind. He does not believe in immortality of any sort beyond the memory of the living. Nor does he believe in a world of self-subsistent essences. At times his terminology may deceive a hasty reader, especially when he writes of "the permanent essence of things," or when he wonders, in telling of the death of Bergotte, where "obligations which have not their sanction in this life" come from. He speculates momentarily about a hypothetical world "entirely different from this, which we leave in order to be born into this world, before perhaps returning to the other to live once again beneath the sway of those unknown laws which we have

obeyed because we bore their precepts in our hearts." This is, however, a thought in passing, and even if he took it seriously, it would
not bear on what to him is the central problem of life, the elusiveness
of the material world. This possible source of the moral virtues is an
interesting problem; it was never his central problem. "We lack the
strength to penetrate to the very depths where truth lies, the real
universe, our authentic impression." Proust cannot convince himself that truth, the real universe, lies anywhere apart from persons
and places, and yet he knows that persons disappear and we leave
places, that time decides the whereabouts of everything.

If it were possible to seize the real in its momentary fullness as it
flashes by, then one might hope to live in the moment. In some
measure this is possible, and if it were not, then memory would have
nothing to revive. But Proust is right in pointing out that no
moment escapes the disintegration of time, and that at no time does
consciousness see things standing still, with their nature neatly
rounded, unified, labeled for all eternity. The idea of existence
which man desires is the conviction that he knows reality as it is,
once for all. As long as we are conscious of the fleeting and flimsy
nature of our own life and of all that surrounds it, our chief impression will be of something missing. "We can sometimes find a person
again, but we cannot abolish time." It is futile and dangerous to
keep on desiring what we cannot have. "We attempt to see the person
whom we love, we ought to attempt not to see her; oblivion alone
brings about an ultimate extinction of desire." Caught between
desire and the fear of oblivion, caught between the futility of desire
and the ceaseless change of all things, the mind nevertheless "strives
for a perception of the mystery that lay hidden in a form or a per-
fume." "Something more lay behind that mobility, that luminos-
ity." At best, experience gives hints of "the real present," "real
presence." Proust distinguishes the present moment from the real
present, and speaks of their fusion. If only the mind could extract
the real present, as it were, "a fragment of time in its pure state,"
then we would at the same time be "our true self," and living "our
true life."

Life as it is usually experienced seems unauthentic, unreal, to Proust. And it is no wonder that he protests that we exist alone. He protests, for he is sure that this is not what life is meant to be, or what life can be if only the mystery of it is revealed. He awaits a revelation. "The visible world is not the true world." There is somewhere, somehow accessible, "a world more real than that in which I lived." He speaks of dedicating his life to "the contemplation of the essence of things," and he means by this "the fixed places," which we ordinarily miss although we constantly desire to know them. Knowing is not looking at, knowing is sympathy, belonging. And "it is in ourselves that we should rather seek to find them. . . . There is no need to travel in order to see it again; we must dig down inwardly to discover it. What once covered the earth is no longer upon it but beneath. . . . We shall see how certain impressions, fugitive and fortuitous, carry us back." If we are to succeed in capturing the authentic impression of life, we must somehow capture it outside time. Time is the implacable enemy of eternity; it is eternity that we live for.

Proust's world is essentially homeless. Man does not and cannot belong to the material world, except temporarily, because it does not have duration or an inherent meaning which is also the meaning for him. His apprehension of reality—and for Proust this world is interchangeable with life or truth—is inevitably full of the anguish of aloneness which can be relieved only by something unexpected. No, that is not quite accurate. Aloneness is not always an agony, it is often boredom. As Bernanos has said, "The world is eaten up by boredom. Such is the true condition of man." Some men are bored because they have never had a vision of life beyond what passes them; they have no sense of life as either purposeful or mysterious. Others, like Proust, are bored because they have had a vision of something beyond or beneath the appearances but have grown tired waiting for what never reveals itself. This boredom is akin to despair, and if it is not actually an agony, it is only because even agony usually becomes weary and listless. Bernanos is not far from Proust when he suggests that "ever since his fall man's condition is such that neither around him nor within him can he perceive anything except in the form of agony." We would only have to add, "or agony that has grown so old that it no longer hurts."

Proustian agony is the agony of unsatisfied desire for a reality which never loses its mystery, in short, a desire for mystery in which the human being can feel enclosed. Instead, the human being is enclosed in himself, surrounded by his desires to break out and be embraced by something or someone which he cannot map or control, and yet by something which recognizes him. "Though I never cease to desire, I never hope." Though I will not hope, I will wait for that which I desire. Any desire expresses some deficiency, and the desire not to be alone expresses a deficiency so basic that life is unendurable without succor or substitution. In the lives of those who are fated not to receive this succor, the satisfaction by memory or desire is at least understandable. In the life of one who will not emerge from himself, but who from behind the peephole of his toy fortress commands the surrounding countryside, such satisfaction need not strike us as quite the last resort that Proust thought it to be. In fact, one of the most persistent evasions of religion is to keep oneself unaware of the questions that it raises about man's illusion of being self-enclosed. At first, this security seems interesting in itself; later, the soul becomes so starved that it must be fed by anything so long as it comes from outside. Proust's hunger was like that, the product of a self-imposed loneliness that did not know communion. But even such a hunger can discover a formula which is the image of eternity.

Perhaps Proust was too pessimistic. He may have exaggerated the hopelessness of his state of being. Certainly, as he himself tells us, there are "days on which the dust of realities is shot with magic sand, on which some trivial incident of life becomes a spring of romance. The whole promontory of the inaccessible world rises clear in the light of our dream, and enters into our life." Even if one has no right to hope, even if we always exist alone and self-enclosed, romance and dreams can break in and introduce us to a different world, the world of a past which feels really present. If we tried to enter this world ourselves, something in us, a weight of some kind, would resist. If we try to make live once more the dream we once had of a real present, "it is a labor in vain to attempt to recapture it. All the efforts of our intellect must prove futile." We would be assuming the existence or the whereabouts of something which does not exist, and "to which we alone can give reality and substance, which we alone can bring into the light of day." But how? "It depends on chance whether we come upon it or not, before we ourselves die."

Chance, not effort, reveals a world more true and real than what we live by. "The past is hidden somewhere outside the realm, beyond the reach of intellect, in some material object." The analogy to grace in Proust's experience is the past as it is released in the memory from its accidental association with some material object. Memory is a vehicle of revelation, and what is revealed is the past which we have already known but not experienced as really present. There is nothing supernatural about chance, nothing divine in the past, and what memory reveals depends on what man longs for as well as on what speaks to him. If he longs only to be spoken to by himself, that speech will be his romance, and his dream will be a dream of a present he should have been capable of experiencing before it became past. The present cannot be apprehended as permanent because it is not whole and it does flee. But whatever is present can be loved in its very impermanence and by this communion given some permanence. To view reality as always outside, to refuse to abandon oneself to it even for a moment, is to reduce experience to self-experience, and revelation to self-revelation. No, this is not revelation; it is narcissism. One does not love the past only because it is a revelation of the really present and mysterious, but because it reveals the mystery of self-experience, our past. And yet no revelation comes when voluntary memory recalls the past; all the details are turned up by force of will, but lack "the idea of existence," or real presence.

Affective, involuntary memory, "the better part of our memory exists outside ourselves, in a platter of rain, in the smell of an unaired room or of the crackling brushwood fire in a cold grate, wherever, in short, we happen upon what our minds, having no use for it, had rejected, the last treasure that the past has in store, the richest, that which when all our flow of tears seems to have dried at the source can make us weep again. Outside ourselves did I say; rather within ourselves, but hidden from our eyes in an oblivion more or less prolonged. It is thanks to this oblivion alone that we can from time to time recover the creature that we were, range ourselves face to face with past events as that creature had to face them, suffer afresh because we are no longer ourselves but he, and because he loved what leaves us now indifferent." The test of revelation, of the authenticity of the real present is its capacity to move us, to "make us weep again." Voluntary memory can make us see, it cannot move us as if we were in communion with someone. Proustian affective memory is mysterious because it does reveal something essentially mysterious; it is reminiscent of what Proust believed man could not have, communion. For only in communion is the whole self moved by someone else. If we could do this to ourselves, we might; but as Proust truthfully admits, we cannot. We must wait until chance, the accident of stumbling over a paving stone or hearing a spoon strike against a plate or tasting the madeleine dipped in tea or smelling the hawthorn in spring, until some such association of memory releases the repressed past in us and it overwhelms us, invades us, knocking down all our resistance so carefully built up out of hurt and fear and theory. The result is, we are moved, and we know the taste of reality for the first time, reality as communion. This is not a Proustian word, but it is only in this experience which Proust would say he did not know, that we can explain to ourselves the effect and the joy of the Proustian revelation of eternity.

And yet we must not forget to distinguish between reality as past and reality as remembered; they are not the same. Proust himself sometimes seems to have forgotten this. He worried about death and old age, mainly because he would no longer be able to remember; the death of others concerned him because with their absence certain associations could no longer be maintained in his memory. "Oblivion" is a word he uses often, and it has a grim sound in each context. But in such an instance as the following, he forgets the plain distinction between real loss and affective loss, between real reality and remembered reality. "On the first night, as I was suffering from cardiac exhaustion, trying to master my pain, I bent . . . but no sooner had I touched the topmost button than my bosom swelled, filled with an unknown, a divine presence. . . . I now recaptured by an instinctive and complete act of recollection, the living reality. That reality has no existence for us, so long as it has not been created anew by our mind." That reality still has no existence for us, and even if one tries to understand resurrection as a phenomenon of memory, it is still true that mental resurrection is not resurrection of the body. To the end, we must insist on the pathos of this distinction, a pathos arising from its finality. No divine presence fills us that is not already there, but a special image of a divine presence appears, in the sense that we have a feeling of presence similar to that which the real presence of the beloved gives the lover. Proust's "living reality," "real presence," "divine presence," are terms which can only be fully applied to a communion in love. If there is no other being whom one can love, if one loves phantoms only, how can we explain the authenticity of the feeling of presence?

This is the most important question that can be asked of Proust's work. "And I begin to ask myself what it could have been, this unremembered state which brought with it no logical proof of its existence, but only the sense that it was happy." Where does "that feeling of happiness" come from, "that happiness, that sense of certainty in happiness?" Augustine had asked the same question. "Where and when had I any experience of happiness that I should remember it and love it and long for it," especially if happiness is "to be joyful in Thee and for Thee and because of Thee, this and no other?" And his answer is that all men desire to have joy in truth. Proust's truth, "our true life," is not life but a similitude of life. Its authenticity comes from the power that desire has to create an image of that which it is made for. Image, or one might better say, a symbol which is delegated authenticity by God in His absence. A desire can create a substitute for its proper end, and the enjoyment of that substitute may be psychologically so much like the enjoyment of the reality missed, that only a person who has experienced both kinds of enjoyment can tell the difference.

Proust's ecstasy after nostalgia dispelled doubt and allayed his anxiety over the future and dread of death. But it did not cure him once for all of fatigue. In fact, as he points out at the end of the series of novels, affective memory engenders a particular kind of fatigue. "There came over me a feeling of profound fatigue at the realization that all this long stretch of time not only had been uninterruptedly lived, thought, secreted by me, that it was my life, my very self, but also that I must every minute of my life, keep it closely by me, that it upheld me, that I was perched on its dizzying summit, that I could not move without carrying it about with me." How different is this sense of fatigue from the exaltation of Augustine. "Thou didst send forth Thy beams and shine upon me and chase away my blindness: Thou didst breath fragrance upon me, and I drew in my breath and do now pant for Thee: I tasted Thee, and now hunger and thirst for Thee; Thou didst touch me, and I have burned for Thy peace." Proust's ecstasy is short-lived: it carries the weight of time within it. This is a way of admitting that one cannot become a "timeless person," but only momentarily feel as if one were. Proust's happiness is the happiness of an "as if" world, where the mind has desperately reached out for substitutes and consecrated them for its desires.

In a world where friendship is a delusion and love always disintegrates before one's eyes, where one cannot forget oneself for even a minute, where confidences have dubious motives, there is no communion and therefore no *real* presence. It may be true, as Proust claims, that man cannot emerge from himself, but the whole point of Proust's gigantic fiction is that man desires to emerge into a world where he can experience true presence. He does not dream true presence, he does not fabricate a society which did not and could not exist. On the contrary, his fiction is plausible precisely because it is a verisimilitude of Proust's personal and social world, a verisimilitude of a world remembered by one who could not find communion within it. Such a remembered state, product of a longing for communion and presence, can supply the feeling of presence. What it cannot supply is the knowledge that there is presence, I for you and you for me. Not even Proust could find the peace that accompanies

real presence. His final judgment on reality is contained in his formula, "The only true paradise is always the paradise we have lost."
This formula would be one-sided and deficient if we were not told
that for Proust the paradise that we have lost is also paradise
regained. And paradise regained is time found again after the long
interior quest for the present which we never enjoyed because it fled
by us so fast and because we were only able to watch it instead of
enjoying it. When we recollect, in the ecstatic and nostalgic moment,
a segment of the past, we find ourselves "in a strange land . . . as
in a stretch of country which we suppose to be strange to us, and
which as a matter of fact we have approached from a new angle,
when after turning out of one road we find ourselves emerging suddenly upon another every inch of which is familiar." This recollection "suddenly brings us a breath of fresh air—refreshing just
because we have breathed it once before—of that purer air which
the poets have vainly tried to establish in Paradise, whereas it could
not convey that profound sensation of renewal if it had not already
been breathed, for the only true paradise . . ." It is customary to
say that we appreciate someone more after he has gone than we did
when he was around. And yet the very character of the appreciation
is a feeling of renewal, of reduplication. We feel as if we have already breathed this air: in truth that is its special and moving
quality. But we know that we have not felt this way before at all,
that until now we have been obdurately closed to that which we
remember with friendliness. We once may have wanted to be
friendly, but did not know how. Paradise regained affords us the
luxury of feeling friendly without having to make any sacrifice. He
who cannot give may still enjoy feeling as if he were giving, and
receiving what he certainly does not deserve. No wonder Proust felt
he was perched on a summit of time, not exactly a time controlled by
him, but a time belonging to him, enclosed within him. And yet he
cannot fool himself completely; paradise is paradise missed and
regained. "We dream much of Paradise, or rather of a number of
successive Paradises, but each of them is, long before we die, a
Paradise lost, in which we should feel ourselves lost too."

THE TWO USES OF MEMORY

Both Augustine and Proust instituted a search that has had profound effects on readers who have followed them. The *Confessions* and the *Recherche* represent interiorized journeys of two powerfully persistent souls, with a common talent for self-analysis that has not been surpassed. If one wants to learn about the external appearance of life in the fourth century, one does not bother with the *Confessions*; for however much there is about Augustine's changing career, his philosophies and his friendships, there is little description of the Italy or North Africa of his day. With Proust it is quite different, he having left an unforgettably vivid and detailed account of the geography, architecture, clothing, manners, and speech of Paris at the turn of the twentieth century. To read Proust, is, in part, to attend a cinema in printed form. To read Augustine, on the other hand, is to listen to man confessing to God. And yet the key to both is their use of memory, and the formula which they shared, the Augustinian expression of which is: "We do not say that we have found what was lost unless we recognize it, nor can we recognize it unless we remember it."

Augustine's disquietude led him to God; Proust's regret led him to himself. Each felt as if he were returning to something once known. In a different sense each was right. Augustine did go back to a God in Christ of whom he had heard in childhood, and Proust recovered a past which he had only glimpsed before it became lost. In another sense, neither one returned at all. Augustine had not known Christ effectively; Proust had failed to enjoy the past when it was present. But they would not have understood their achievement had they not seen something in it, for Augustine, what he had just begun to hear about, for Proust, what he had wanted to imagine. Proust's slightly different formula which says that the only true paradise is the paradise that we have lost does not apply to Augustine at all, and must be superimposed on the Augustinian formula of recognition in order to give the full flavor of the Proustian taste of the real. Augustine's disquietude led to much wandering, away from God, it is true, but away from a God that he had never gone very near. Proust's journey started out in the middle of time, the present, where he had missed the point, failed to consummate what it had offered. If Augustine had fled from God, Proust was too much a prisoner to move at all.

Much of the imagery of the *Confessions* refers to a journey, a wandering, the twisting and turning of a man who physically and intellectually was never still. We know that Proust's journey was accomplished in the cork-lined room where he lived for years. Augustine, unlike Proust, did not live in the past, he had too much to think about and do. Proust was not interested in the future, because he knew it presented the same unbeatable challenge as the present, the imprisoning of a man who could not or would not emerge from himself. Only in the affective, involuntary intuition of the past was he to live in a world where he was free. Proust wanted to be released from time, or so he thought. But it was not time which was his jailor, only his own inability to forget himself. It is curious that a man who possessed himself and himself alone should be obsessed by the loss of his past, rather than by his loss of reality outside himself. This is, however, the meaning of a preoccupation with time lost rather than reality lost.

The world of Proust is a world to be written about, not loved; only the viewer will be missed and missed only by himself. It is a world in which a sense of identity depends on the chance that some association with the past, with the world and oneself, will be resurrected by sensation. It is a world where one is at the mercy not of time but of matter and memory. It is a frightening as well as a fascinating world; the fascination is built on a horror of aloneness and death that is never completely exorcised. To the end the Proustian man must drag the heavy weight of his time with him. It is a weight rather than a depth that he has been preoccupied with, a burden not a dimension. What sets him apart from Augustine, the religious mind in essence, is the profundity of Augustine's belonging to God. His disquietude led him to an understanding of himself, where he belonged, the Church. It was transformed into self-control and rest. But he was not looking for himself; he was looking for something surer, Truth. The result was he found God and then, only then, found himself. "For where I found truth, there I found my God, who is Truth itself." And what more can a man know of himself than that his heart will be restless until its rests in God? For Augustine home is where the heart is, and the heart is with God. For Proust home is simply Combray. There is an important difference between the ways in which Augustine and Proust used memory, the former as a vehicle of grace, the latter as a vehicle of chance. There is an even more important difference between what each remembers; the former remembers God, the latter remembers only his own past. For Proust to remember is to make a journey backwards; to live is to take this journey, to live is to remember. For Augustine to remember is to return from one's moral and intellectual wanderings; to live is to recognize Christ. For Proust the Way is art, the marshaling of the debris of nostalgia. For Augustine the Way is humility, the learning of the Incarnation.

Both Augustine and Proust knew the joy of remembering what we have never really known; this is the formula of their common humanity. One is tempted to say of Proust, "He lacked the power for the vision of God, but not the power for the vision of man." But the vision of man is incomplete—this is the Augustinian wisdom—without the vision of God. Distorted though the image may be, it reflects its Creator; this is the significance of the sense Proust had that in the nostalgic vision he experienced all that mattered, life, truth, the real, eternity. "We are men," Augustine said, "created in the image of our Creator, whose eternity is true and whose truth is eternal . . . let us, like that younger son of the gospel come to ourselves, and arise and return to Him from whom by our sin we had departed."

THE SEVENTH SOLITUDE
*Man's Isolation in Kierkegaard,
Dostoevsky, and Nietzsche*
BY RALPH HARPER

designer:	Athena Blackorby
typesetter:	Baltimore Type and Composition Co.
typefaces:	Bodoni Book, Mademoiselle
printer:	J. H. Furst & Co.
paper:	Perkins and Squier, SM
binder:	Moore & Co.
cover material:	Holliston's Roxite C